D0428746

# THE 160-CHARACTER SOLUTION

# THE 160-CHARACTER SOLUTION

How Text Messaging and
Other Behavioral Strategies
Can Improve Education

..............................

BENJAMIN L. CASTLEMAN

JOHNS HOPKINS

UNIVERSITY PRESS

Baltimore

© 2015 Johns Hopkins University Press
All rights reserved. Published 2015
Printed in the United States of America on acid-free paper
9 8 7 6 5 4 3 2 1

Johns Hopkins University Press
2715 North Charles Street
Baltimore, Maryland 21218-4363
www.press.jhu.edu

Library of Congess Cataloguing in Publication Data
Castleman, Benjamin L.
The 160-character solution : how text messaging and other behavioral strategies
can improve education / Benjamin L. Castleman.
    pages cm
Includes bibliographical references and index.
ISBN 978-1-4214-1874-2 (hardcover : alk. paper) — ISBN 978-1-4214-1875-9
(electronic) — ISBN 1-4214-1874-6 (hardcover : alk. paper) — ISBN 1-4214-1875-4
(electronic)  1. School improvement programs—United States. 2. Educational
change—United States. 3. Academic achievement—Psychological aspects.
4. Educational psychology. 5. Rational choice theory. 6. Decision making.
7. Education—Aims and objectives—United States. 8. Education and state—
United States. 9. Educational equalization—United States. I. Title.
LB2822.82.C378 2015
371.2′070973—dc23    2015010632

A catalog record for this book is available from the British Library.

Special discounts are available for bulk purchases of this book.
For more information, please contact Special Sales at 410-516-6936
or specialsales@press.jhu.edu.

Johns Hopkins University Press uses environmentally friendly
book materials, including recycled text paper that is composed
of at least 30 percent post-consumer waste, whenever possible.

To my grandparents,

LEONARD and ANITA CASTLEMAN,

whose high expectations and even stronger love

provided the foundation on which this book and all

else I have achieved have been built

# Contents

Introduction
. . . . . . . . . . . . . . . . .
Decisions, Decisions

HARVARD UNIVERSITY IS HOME to some of the most talented students in the world. Admitted freshmen often have amassed accomplishments by the age of eighteen which many of us would be hard-pressed to match over the course of our lifetimes (yours truly included): scientific patents; orchestral performances with world-famous musicians; the creation of tech startup companies or multinational nonprofit organizations. Especially as Harvard has expanded its need-based financial aid, the university is also home to incredibly bright students who have overcome daunting adversity in their lives: students who participated in national science competitions and attained near-perfect SAT scores despite being homeless throughout high school; undocumented students who arrived in the United States as teenagers and who excelled in school at the same time that they were working to support their families, serving as translators for their parents, and taking care of younger siblings.

Harvard is also home to a tremendous array of support resources to ensure that all students achieve academic success. These include graduate student and university staff who serve as residential advisors in every freshmen dorm, faculty advisors, peer advisors, tutoring and writing centers—all of this in addition to the many instructional resources offered by each academic department.

And yet, even at a university so infused with natural talent, achievement, and comprehensive supports, incoming students sometimes struggle to make informed decisions about the educational pathway they pursue. I witnessed this firsthand; for four years I served as a residential advisor (or freshman proctor, in Harvard-speak) while completing my own doctoral work. At the beginning of every academic year I would meet with all the students in my Grays Hall entryway to discuss the courses they would take during the fall semester. What struck me every year was the vast diversity of life experiences among the twenty-seven young people living within this single entryway at Harvard. We had direct descendants of the Founding Fathers, whose parents and brothers and cousins had attended the university for untold generations. In the same suite as them were students who were the first in their family to complete high school—let alone college—and who had bounced among various shelters for most of their high school career.

Some students would come into these advising meetings having scoured the course catalog and generated a ranked list of the twenty-five courses they would explore during the first semester. But a surprising number of students had a much more difficult time choosing their courses. The sheer wealth of options—everything from Sanskrit to biomedical engineering—was intimidating for some. Others had a hard time determining which course level was appropriate for freshmen (since every department had its own approach to course numbering) or deciding how to balance required courses, major prerequisites, and intellectually stimulating electives.

More often than not these decisions were particularly challenging for students from lower-income backgrounds or who were the first in their family to go to college. Students from college-educated families had spent hours over the summer looking over the course catalog with their parents. Low-income and first-generation students' parents were in some cases reluctant to provide any guidance, for lack of personal experience choosing college courses. In other instances these parents provided their children with guidance that had a certain logic (for example, "get all of your requirements out of the way freshman year"), but which stood in contrast to Harvard's advising philosophy.

Lacking access to informed familial guidance and in the midst of transitioning to a world that was profoundly different from their home communities, students often resorted to simplifying strategies to make decisions. One student took a full load of premed requirements because her extended family had always wanted her to be a doctor, despite the fact that her interests were mainly in politics and government. Several students decided to take a popular course called the Science of Cooking, not because they had any interest in science or cooking, but rather because they had friends enrolling in the course. Others were drawn to courses featuring material from popular culture (HBO's show *The Wire*, for instance) even if they lacked interest in the underlying disciplinary lens through which the pop culture material would be analyzed.

Some might say that the challenge of finding one's intellectual pathway is part of the collegiate experience. But in my experience as a residential advisor, these simplifying strategies for choosing classes often led students into courses that were not aligned with their academic interests or goals. This, in turn, resulted in lower grades and heightened stress and anxiety. For some of the low-income or first-generation students, frustration and dissatisfaction with courses exacerbated the cultural and psychological challenges of fitting into the Harvard community. Most students eventually found their footing and thrived at the university. For many, however, the challenge of choosing courses contributed to an emotionally wrought freshman year.

As my work has focused on student and parent decision making in education, I often think back to these advising conversations. If students at the most highly endowed university in the world struggle with complex decisions, imagine what it's like for students and families in underresourced communities to make decisions about their own education.

## A PERPLEXING PROBLEM IN AMERICAN PUBLIC EDUCATION

My interest in decision making in education is largely motivated by a decades-long dilemma facing educators, researchers, and policy makers. On the one hand, we have made substantial resource investments to improve the quality of education for all children, with a particular emphasis on strengthening educational programs and pathways for students from economically disadvantaged backgrounds. To ensure that all children have access to a quality early childhood education, numerous cities and states have invested in universal prekindergarten programs. Through Title I funding, the federal government has provided schools serving lower-income students with over $15 billion in supplementary funds to reduce class sizes, expand class time, and provide more professional development for teachers (U.S. Department of Education, 2014; U.S. Government Accountability Office, 2011). And over the past several decades both the federal and state governments have invested hundreds of billions of dollars in need-based financial aid to increase college affordability for low-income students (Baum, Ma, & Payea, 2013).

More recently, local, state, and federal governments have also expanded the amount of publicly available information about school quality at every level of education. In fact, when it comes to finding quality schooling options for our children, parents have never had so much information at their fingertips. Any parent with an Internet connection—or even just a smartphone—can access a wealth of information about schools in their community. In many states, parents of preschool-age children can access Quality Rating Information Systems to learn about various dimensions of early child care center quality, ranging from the safety of the physical environment and the amount of professional development staff have received to the ways in which center staff engage and support new families. Parents of elementary- or middle-school-age children can often read school report cards that provide detailed information about student academic achievement, disciplinary issues, and teacher qualifications. High school students and their families can obtain extensive information about postsecondary options—how much financial aid the family is likely to qualify for, the academic and extracurricular programs that each college offers, and in some states even how much the student is likely to earn if they graduate from a particular institution or program.

The availability of such rich information about school quality represents remarkable progress from even a decade or two ago, when preschool choice was largely informed by word-of-mouth advice from friends in your neighborhood. The elementary school students attended was primarily determined by where they lived. For college-bound kids, their search began by leafing through guides that were thicker than phone books or perusing the stack of glossy college admissions flyers at the school library.

Despite these resources and the proliferation of information, profound inequalities still exist in education—and in some cases, have even widened considerably over time. This is true among children too young for formal schooling—76 percent of four-year-olds from the top income quintile attend preschool, compared with only 50 percent of four-year-old children from families in the lowest income quintile (Cascio & Schanzenbach, 2014)—and continues up through the educational pipeline and into postsecondary education. Among the highest-achieving students in the country, only 34 percent of the lowest-income students attend a selective college or university, compared with 78 percent of their high-income peers (Hoxby & Avery, 2012).

With these substantial resources and the overwhelming amount of information, why haven't we been able to do more to reduce these educational disparities? In this book I make the case that chipping away at these inequalities will require more than just additional resources and information. What we need is greater attention to how students and their families make decisions about their educational options.

## NEW INSIGHTS INTO DECISION MAKING

Policy makers think about families making education decisions in the same way that stockbrokers pick mutual funds. Successful brokers typically don't have an emotional attachment to one stock over another. They analyze the benefits and risks associated with various investments and select the option that maximizes the return for their clients. Educational choice policies in this country have been designed around the belief that families take a similar cost-benefit approach to evaluating school options. They consider the various schools available—whether preschools in their community or colleges their child has a good chance of being accepted to—and choose the one that maximizes learning and achievement relative to the cost of attendance at that school.

Information clearly plays a role in this model of decision making. In order to make informed schooling choices, students and parents have to know about all of the available schooling options and have a comprehensive understanding of what each school has to offer—everything from instructional quality and classroom environment to peer influences and school safety. They also have to be aware of the costs associated with each option—not only out-of-pocket expenses, such as tuition, but also *effort costs*, like the time they'd have to spend on the bus or in the car to get their child to and from school.

How can we explain this persistence of inequalities in education? One reason could be that families just don't have enough information about the variation in the quality of available schools. If parents don't know that these options exist, providing better information about school quality should be an effective solution for reducing disparities. After all, stockbrokers need sound financial analyses and earnings reports to make informed decisions about which stocks to pick. By the same logic, the increase in school information should allow parents to identify the best schools for their children, regardless of where they live or how much they earn.

This idea of information as a powerful equalizer in education has an intoxicating appeal to policy makers. As local and state governments have fewer resources for public education, the idea of providing good information looks cheap, easy, and popular. Many people, when surveyed, strongly support the idea of having more options rather than fewer, whether in education, health care, or renewable energy (DiPerna, 2014; Keckley & Coughlin, 2012; Solar City, 2014). Informational campaigns encouraging lower-income students to attend better schools are often far more cost-effective and politically feasible than resource-intensive efforts to improve the quality of schools these students currently attend. Finally, there is a deceptively simple "if you build it, they will come" logic behind information-oriented policies. Many campaigns to provide families with better school information focus most of their efforts on getting information into the public domain (for example, printing school report cards, creating a college search engine), on the belief that people will find the information, know how to interpret it, and make more informed decisions about the educational pathways they pursue.

## THE CHALLENGE OF DECISION MAKING

Unfortunately, most of us rarely make decisions the way stockbrokers do—by weighing the benefits and costs. Even when we have access to a wealth of information to aid our decision making, we get stuck. Take, for instance, the process of purchasing a car. Next to buying a home or paying for college, cars are one of the primary investments that we make. It is also a purchase for which there is a tremendous volume of information available. From *Consumer Reports* to *Kelley Blue Book* and thousands of websites, there is an endless supply of information to help guide people to a car that meets their needs. Whether one values fuel efficiency, sporty handling, or room to lug around kids and their gear, with a little online browsing a buyer can find ratings of every car on the market. Yes, setting aside a few hours for this kind of exhaustive search isn't always easy given how busy we are, but what's a few hours weighed against the cost of a car purchase? Yet, many of us buy a car based on much more superficial factors (Ariely, 2008).

I encountered this situation recently when visiting my ninety-two-year-old grandmother. She of all people should make informed decisions about cars. She reads voraciously, visits the library several times a week, and has all the time in the world to research cars. And yet, her views about which cars are reliable or not are heavily influenced by her friends' experiences. "Those Hondas are no good!" she told me. "Ethel[1] had to have two brake jobs last year alone. They just don't build those cars well." It never occurred to my grandmother that the brake jobs might have had something to do with how Ethel drove—she has written off an entire line of cars because of one friend's trips to the mechanic. My grandmother is by no means alone in this. Evaluating a multitude of options across various dimensions turns out to be challenging for most people. Faced with such complexity, many of us use simplifying strategies to guide our decisions.

Or consider the challenge that many of us face getting regular exercise. Seventy-five percent of Americans recognize that exercise is important, and for many people, their New Year's resolution is to exercise more regularly (PR Newswire, 2006; Rasmussen Reports, 2011). By any calculation the benefits of exercise clearly swamp the costs. People who work out regularly have a reduced likelihood of heart disease or stroke, are less likely to get injured, and tend to have better mental health (U.S. Department of Health and Human Services, 2014a). For most people the cost of exercising can be as little as thirty or forty-five minutes every few days to take a jog, or $50 a month to join a gym. And yet, many of us struggle to follow through on our intentions to exercise on a regular basis. The alarm clock goes off in the morning, but we hit the snooze button a few times rather than go for a run. Even our best intentions are foiled. We sign up for a gym membership and plan to go during our lunch break, but weeks go by without us actually making it out of the office. Our future selves recognize the many benefits that come from regular exercise, but our present selves want the extra sleep and leisurely lunch.[2] Our tendency to be swayed by the present even when it comes at the expense of something we want in the future affects not just whether we exercise, of course, but also whether we successfully stick to a diet, are able to quit smoking, or set aside money for retirement, as well as many other good intentions.

My own thinking about the challenge of decision making was inspired initially not by a book, lecture, or journal article, but rather by the experience of taking my children to toy stores. Lila is six and Simon is four. Like just about every other kid in America, they love toy stores, or at least the idea of toy stores. We live in Charlottesville, Virginia, where there is a beautiful ten-block pedestrian mall downtown. We spend a lot of time on the mall, riding the carousel, going to the children's museum, shopping at the farmer's market, seeing concerts at the outdoor pavilion. There are also two toy stores on the mall, and whenever we walk past one of them, it's like there's an invisible magnetic force pulling them inside. Most of the time my wife and I keep a steady onward pace, firmly gripping Lila's and Simon's hands lest they make a beeline for the toy store entrance. Every once in a while, though, we relent and go inside. On these occasions they shriek with joy and dash inside, imaginations running amok with all the toys they'll soon encounter.

And that's typically when the fun starts to fade—at least for my wife and me. After redirecting them from the expensive construction vehicles and play sets, our kids usually settle on the more reasonably priced LEGO and action figure sections of the store. Then the interminable pacing starts. Back and forth they go from one toy to the next, picking up and closely examining each package, trying to decide whether to get a Ninja Turtles LEGO set or roaring T-Rex or singing Sophia the First doll. It's like they're scrutinizing diamonds, trying to determine which has the best cut and greatest clarity. What we've realized over time is that, faced with so many choices, they can't make any choice at all. What they eventually wind up getting is usually just a function of what happens to be in their hand when my wife or I insists that it's time to leave the store.

The experience of watching my kids struggle in the face of so many choices at the toy store reminded me of a time I spent earlier in my career as a high school teacher in Providence, Rhode Island, helping students apply to college. Our school served primarily low-income students who would be the first in their family to go to college. Because families lacked the resources and experience to help their child explore a range of colleges, we integrated the college and financial aid application process into the senior year curriculum. There was one student in particular whose college search stands out to me.

Vince was a hard-working, conscientious, and charismatic student who by senior year had a solid transcript and an impressive set of internships in the community. His college entrance exam scores were on the low side, but his application was still competitive at a range of colleges and universities. Vince lived with his mother, who had come to the United States just before he was born, and his younger sister. Vince's mom cared deeply about his education but felt ill prepared to provide much in the way of guidance. She had finished high school in her home country but never had the chance to go to college and didn't feel like she understood the higher education system in the United States. She worked at a university, however, that offered an employee benefit that would pay $10,000 per year toward Vince's education. She was determined to help Vince find a college where this contribution, combined with what she had saved, would be enough to cover tuition and fees.

Early in his senior year Vince and I sat down to discuss which colleges he might apply to. I suggested a combination of public and private institutions in the Providence area, knowing that Vince was very close to his family and that his mother would probably want him to stay close to home. Vince, however, had a much different vision for where he would apply to college. "I'm applying to just two schools," Vince told me. "University of Miami and Harvard. Whichever I get into, I'm going to walk on to the football team and play linebacker." Never mind that Vince was 120 pounds tops and hadn't played football since fifth grade—he was entirely serious about his college intentions. Even when I pointed out that he might have trouble making the football team when there were guys three times his size and five times as fast, Vince remained undeterred. "Even if I can't play football I want to be at a school where there's a top ten football team—and man, Miami Beach! And Harvard, that's like the best college in the world." Vince had decidedly more negative views about the local community college and four-year public university. "All those kids drop out after like three weeks. Why would I go there?"

Vince wasn't being glib about his postsecondary plans—he just was basing his application plans on what he knew about college, which was largely informed by college football and Harvard's omnipresent brand name. No one in his extended family had gone to college, and the few people in his neighborhood who had started out at one of the local college options hadn't lasted through the fall semester. Vince's mother was also skeptical about Miami and Harvard but didn't know where else to suggest that he apply.

Vince was fortunate to be at a high school where students had access to individualized college advising and help with the financial aid process. He did wind up applying to both Miami and Harvard, neither of which accepted him, but also to several local postsecondary options, one of which he enrolled at in the year following high school. Absent this individualized guidance through the college search and application process, however, it's unlikely that Vince would have found a college option that matched his academic performance and that he could afford.

## BEHAVIORAL INSIGHTS INTO DECISION MAKING

Of course, it's not just young children or students like Vince who find complex choices and complicated decisions challenging. Most of us struggle with making fully informed decisions or following through on intentions we have set for ourselves. What is particularly striking is how seemingly small differences in how decisions are presented can have a profound influence on our actions:

- The number of choices with which we are presented (like the number of action figures on a toy shelf) impacts what we choose or whether we make any choice at all. For instance, doctors are much more likely to prescribe a course of treatment when they are presented with one option rather than two possible treatments (Redelmeier & Shafir, 1995).
- The way information is delivered or framed influences how we respond. Sending college freshmen text message reminders about renewing their financial aid, for example, in addition to the e-mail-based reminders they already receive from the U.S. Department of Education, increases the probability that community college students persist in college by almost 20 percent (Castleman & Page, forthcoming).
- Informing people about how their actions compare to the norm can lead people to make substantial adjustments to their behaviors. Sending people postcards that report their home energy usage

compared with their neighbors' leads households to reduce energy consumption (Allcott, 2011).

- Eliminating small up-front fees increases the likelihood that people will be willing to make substantial financial investments. Getting rid of a $6 fee associated with sending college entrance exams to additional colleges increases attendance at four-year institutions (Pallais, forthcoming).

Underlying these responses to small changes in how decisions are presented is a fairly common set of behavioral reactions that people have when presented with complex choices, confusing information, and complicated processes. For instance, sorting through a wide array of choices is a cognitively challenging task, especially when the choices differ on many dimensions. As a result, many of us put off these choices or use some kind of simplifying rule to make a decision—often simplifying the decision in a way that may be unrelated to the outcome we're actually striving for. Reducing the number of choices people face reduces the cognitive burden and allows us to make more informed choices about what we want. Or, as many of us find when it comes time to exercise, our present desires (more sleep, avoidance of physical discomfort, etc.) often reign supreme—even when they are in direct conflict with the goals we have set for our future selves. One implication of this bias toward the present is that many of us struggle to set aside time or attention to deal with onerous near-term tasks even when we recognize that they are essential to realizing our longer-term intentions. Providing people with prompts and encouragement to complete these tasks can make a substantial difference in whether they follow through on their intentions.

Each chapter of this book is organized around a different set of concrete strategies and approaches to help people make more informed decisions, follow through on their intentions, and achieve their full potential in education. Within each chapter, I provide a concise and intuitive description of relevant behavioral obstacles that can interfere with people making informed decisions, along with concrete illustrations of how these behavioral responses arise and have been addressed in other policy settings. Next, I look at promising interventions that have already been designed and tested to help people make more informed educational decisions in the face of these behavioral challenges. Finally, I explore additional solutions that can further improve students' educational achievement.

### APPLYING BEHAVIORAL INSIGHTS TO IMPROVE EDUCATION

This book is *not* intended to provide a comprehensive explanation of all the key principles from psychology, behavioral economics, marketing, and neuroscience which inform what we know about how people make decisions. Rather, I draw from a very strong foundation of prior works that have translated rigorous research in these fields into decision-making concepts that are more easily grasped by a popular audience. These books include *Nudge*, by Richard Thaler and Cass Sunstein; *Thinking, Fast and Slow*, by Daniel Kahneman; and *Predictably Irrational*, by Dan Ariely. For readers who want a more thorough discussion of the science of decision making, I highly recommend consulting these books and even some of the TED Talks that describe each approach.

The contribution I hope to make is in helping readers understand how behavioral obstacles may contribute to persistent socioeconomic inequalities in educational achievement and education; even more importantly, I identify strategies that apply behavioral insights to support students and families in making more informed decisions that may ultimately lead them to better outcomes.

A question readers may ask at this point is, why focus on decision making? Why behavioral solutions to educational problems? Shouldn't we be investing in high-quality early childhood education for all, better teachers for all classrooms, and increased college affordability for all families? The simple answer is that of course we should continue to advocate for these policies. Yet these investments require systemic, long-term change and extensive public investment. At the same time that we continue to pursue progress in these domains, behavioral solutions focused on improving student and family decision making are low cost, are easily scaled, and can directly impact the education of students *now*.

One reason to invest in behavioral strategies to support more informed decision making in education is that, simply put, behavioral solutions are all around us. Many of these solutions have emerged from other public policy sectors, such as financial planning and public health. I provide numerous examples of these interventions in the chapters that follow. But an even broader set of strategies can be drawn from the private sector. After all, what else is advertising but a strategic set of efforts to influence our decisions about what we buy?

I first recognized the many lessons to be learned from advertising and marketing science when I was writing a white paper for the Gates Foundation on how behavioral insights could be applied to improve the design and delivery of college and financial aid information. I was writing about many of the solutions I discuss in detail in this book:

- simplifying information to reduce students' and families' sense of being overwhelmed with the sheer volume and complexity of postsecondary information;
- providing additional structure and sequence to information to help students know which college attributes to prioritize over others during their search;
- providing personalized prompts and encouragement so that students do not miss important college and financial aid application deadlines;
- facilitating access to individualized college and financial aid advising when students encounter obstacles they can't overcome on their own.

I was reminded of this recently when I was doing my taxes. Here was TurboTax on my computer screen, applying the same techniques I was writing about for the Gates paper. Gone were the days of staring at complex and confusing income tax forms, vainly trying to figure out how to get started or what each field was even asking for in the first place. TurboTax presented me with one question at a time, using gentle, conversational language that made me feel like my uncle was in the room, patiently guiding me through the process. TurboTax devoted more time and attention to common topics, such as property tax deductions, and moved quickly through less common items. And individualized help from a tax professional was always just a click away, through live chat or a user's forum.

This was an epiphany moment for me: behavioral interventions were everywhere, and they have been for at least a half century—or whenever ad men like those portrayed on *Mad Men* first appeared—quietly guiding what we buy, how we shop, even what we value. Why not repurpose these same strategies to help students and families make more informed decisions about their educational choices?

The potential power of behavioral solutions notwithstanding, I am sensitive to concerns we may have about wading into the murky territory of influencing the decisions people make. Independence from government intrusion is a right that many Americans cherish, even more so in the wake of recent revelations about data gathered by the National Security Agency. In light of my goal to use behavioral strategies to reduce inequalities in education, this is particularly fraught ground since I advocate targeting these behavioral interventions toward students from economically disadvantaged backgrounds. Before proceeding then, I should make several explicit points about the types of intervention I propose.

First, the consideration is not *whether* to influence the decisions students and families make, but rather whether we can *improve* on the current ways that we influence these decisions. Various factors already guide students toward certain behaviors. For instance, complicated information about student loan repayment options makes it more likely that borrowers will just stick with the standard loan repayment plan in which they are automatically enrolled. Providing borrowers with simplified information about loan repayment options is not then introducing influence on decision making where it did not previously exist, but rather presenting information in a way that enables borrowers to make more informed choices.

Second, I am not advocating that educators or policy makers tell people which educational opportunities they should pursue, but rather that we present options in a way that allows people to make decisions about schooling options which align best with the goals they would set for themselves. Proactively giving parents information about how their child is doing in school is not telling them how to be involved in their child's education, but instead allowing them to determine their level of involvement with more concrete and personalized information about their child's performance. Throughout the book I advocate for strategies that allow students and families to make informed decisions and that help them to follow through on intentions they have set for themselves. I don't recommend interventions that assume to tell people what is in their own best interest.

Finally, and perhaps most importantly, I am not implicitly assuming that lower-income students or their parents are in any way less innately capable or determined to make well-informed decisions about their educational pathways. In nearly fifteen years as a teacher, school administrator, and educational researcher focused on improving postsecondary outcomes for low-income students, I know from firsthand experience that intelligence, tenacity, and drive can be found in equal measure across the socioeconomic spectrum. Rather, challenges that economically disadvantaged students and their families face in making educational decisions stem from lack of personal or familial experience with key educational investments, lack of access to social or professional circles to which students and families can turn for informed guidance, and, as I discuss in the next chapter, very real impediments that poverty can introduce into the decision-making process.

## THE PROMISE AND POTENTIAL OF BEHAVIORAL INTERVENTION

A final word before I forge ahead: strategies that support students to make more informed educational decisions have the potential to generate returns that are many magnitudes greater than their cost to implement. From preschool through graduate school, students and their families encounter a series of decision-making crossroads that can determine whether they progress into lower-quality or higher-quality educational environments. In some cases higher-quality educational opportunities simply aren't available to students, in which case there really isn't a decision to be made. But in other communities, informational and behavioral bottlenecks stand between students and higher-quality schooling. For instance, whether lower-income students attend a better middle school or not is affected by the length and complexity of the booklet that describes available school choices. Whether college-ready students actually enter college is often influenced by whether they think students "like them" go to and succeed in college.

Take a three-year-old girl living in Providence, Rhode Island. Over the course of her early life, she and her family will face a series of important and consequential decisions in education: which preschool and elementary school to attend; which middle and high school courses to take; whether to register for the SAT or apply for financial aid. What if, at each cross-roads, we were able to nudge her into better schools—from early childhood education through primary and secondary schooling and on into college? What if we could provide simplified information about course pathways that would position her for college-level work? What if we could help her family navigate complex financial aid applications to make sure they receive as much financial assistance as possible to apply toward the cost of college? What would her educational outcomes look like compared with those of another three-year-old in Providence who didn't receive these nudges?

Think of behavioral interventions as a way of breaking through the decision-making bottlenecks that students and families confront at each of these crossroads. At each critical juncture, by supporting students and families to make informed decisions about the educational options they pursue, we can help them choose paths that lead to greater success. Imagine if we are able to do this at every important crossroad. Where the student winds up is likely to be very different than where they began, and also fundamentally different from where they would have traveled to without targeted assistance navigating the complicated processes that arise at every stage. These interventions need not cost much—some of the behavioral interventions I describe in the book cost as little as a few dollars per student—but can generate lasting and profound effects on the course of students' educational life.

## Chapter 1

. . . . . . . . . . . . . . . .

## The Cost of Complexity

THINK ABOUT A COMPLEX ASSIGNMENT you needed to complete at school or work—a final paper for a class, an end-of-year report on a project you manage, or a book on behavioral insights and education which you've committed to write. Months before the assignment is due, most of us feel quite confident that it will get done. If you're forward planning like me, you might even block out large chunks of time in your calendar each week to space out when you work on it. You have lots of ideas for what you want to say, so it's really only a matter of putting it down on paper. With time on your side, there's little to worry about.

However, each week those chunks of time you set aside to work on the assignment seem to vanish right before your eyes. There were meetings and phone calls you had to schedule, a spur-of-the-moment lunch with your spouse which you didn't want to pass up, that World Cup game between the United States and Germany determining who would go forward to the knockout round. But there's always next week . . . until next week arrives, and the time you've set aside to work on the assignment is somehow much smaller than you intended.

Even when we successfully set aside time to work on these complex assignments, we often struggle to maintain as much focus and attention as we would ideally intend. There are e-mails to answer, new tweets to read, people to talk to at work. Out of the two or three hours we've set aside to really dive into the assignment, many of us have a hard time working for more than fifteen or twenty minutes without distraction. An entire industry has cropped up to address this problem. Some tools, like Freedom, allow users to voluntarily block Internet access for eight hours at a time so that you have no choice but to hunker down and write. Others, like Anti-Social, are more selective, blocking access to social media sites like Facebook and Twitter but allowing access to less distracting web content.

Of course, for these tools to be successful, people have to choose to make use of them. Especially when faced with important assignments and dwindling time with which to complete them, the choice seems obvious and straightforward: "I need to complete this assignment. Completing this assignment is going to take some time. I know I get distracted by my e-mail and Twitter. Therefore, in the time I set aside to work on this assignment, I will use Freedom or Anti-Social to keep me from getting distracted." As logical as this seems, however, many people struggle to avoid the temptation that online distraction offers—yours truly included.

There's a certain poetic justice in the fact that as I write a book about behavioral insights and education, I find myself constantly reflecting on my own difficulties setting aside time to write or staying focused during the time blocks I set aside. Take today as an illustration: I intended to set aside the entire day to write, but there were three different pressing phone calls I had to schedule (one with my editor), which cut my writing time down to a few hours. At least I had a two-hour block this morning—but within that time, I've probably checked my e-mail or Twitter at least fifty times. I could block access to these sites—I know I *should* block access to help me focus—but the temptation of the new message or new social media post is too great to deny myself the immediate gratification.

### THE COGNITIVE DEMANDS OF COMPLEX TASKS AND INFORMATION

Many of the behavioral responses that interfere with people's ability to make fully informed decisions stem from this basic challenge: complex tasks and complex information require us to invest substantial cognitive energy in the form of attention. Yet our ability to invest this attention and energy is at constant odds with our tendency to respond to more immediately gratifying impulses and stimuli. To understand this tension between cognitively demanding tasks and our propensity to gravitate toward more distracting stimuli we encounter, it is helpful to take a quick tour of the neurology of decision making. As I said in the introduction, my goal in this book is not to provide a comprehensive synthesis of the underlying neurology and psychology that impact how we approach complicated decisions, but rather to give readers an intuitive grasp of these concepts which they can then apply to thinking about decision making in education. Much of what I cover in the next several paragraphs draws on Daniel Kahneman's highly illuminating book *Thinking, Fast and Slow*.

For each of us, the process of making decisions is largely governed by two primary systems within our brain. Think of one system as your brain's accelerator.[1] This system generates our immediate responses, impulses, and emotional reactions. When the dessert tray rolls by in a restaurant, the accelerator hits the floor and tells us that we want something sweet. Think of the other system as your brain's brake. This system is responsible for logical analysis, careful deliberations, and conscious reflection. This is the part of our brain that says, "But aren't you trying to watch what you eat?" in response to our immediate desire for chocolate cake.

The rational view of decision making is one of impartial cost-benefit analysis: we are presented with multiple options, we patiently assess the benefits and costs associated with each option, and we choose the option that maximizes the benefits relative to the costs. In the context of education, think of someone evaluating day care alternatives for their children. Their choices might be (a) a parent or relative stays home with the child, (b) the family hires a nanny, or (c) the family sends the child to one of several different day care centers. In the traditional decision-making model, each family would comprehensively weigh what each alternative has to offer and then choose the day care option that maximizes the family's well-being relative to the costs, broadly speaking, of pursuing that path.

We have come to learn, however, that the deliberative region of our brains does not exert as much control as one might hope with consequential decisions. In fact, the impulsive system is often covertly at work, shaping our decisions in ways we are not always conscious of. I described one example of our impulsive system's influence at the start of the chapter. When we are presented with immediate and attention-grabbing stimuli—like Twitter notifications—our brain's accelerator revs into action, drawing our attention away from the activity on which we are trying to concentrate and toward the new and alluring piece of information. This response is, of course, quite useful in many instances. We often *want* our minds to focus on new stimuli, such as when a car is about to veer into our lane on the highway. But new stimuli can also be quite distracting.

Another way our impulsive system affects our decision making is by streamlining how we respond to complex information or complicated processes. In the introduction I talked about how my grandmother's assessment of cars is largely shaped by her friends' experiences with their own vehicles. If a friend's car requires a lot of work (regardless of whether that friend's driving might be the cause), my grandmother concludes that there's something wrong with the entire brand of cars. Her impulsive system is enabling her to boil down a very challenging and mentally demanding analysis of what different makes and models have to offer to a very simple decision rule: Ethel's Honda required a lot of work; therefore, all Hondas are bad.

The impulsive system's influence on our decision making arises as well in education. Take, for example, the process by which families discern which colleges would provide affordable postsecondary pathways for their child. This is a very complicated analysis for most families. There are the listed tuition and fees, or sticker price, that colleges publicize, but many students are eligible for some combination of institutional, state, and federal grants and loans. This aid can lead to a very different—and often much lower—net price. Furthermore, the net price students face often varies considerably from one college to the next, depending on the institutional and state grants and scholarships for which the student might qualify, and from one student to the next, depending on their individual financial situation. While the federal government has invested in a variety of tools to help families get estimates of their net price at a given college, students and parents without college experience—or without recent college experience—may be unaware that these tools exist. The complexity of estimating the net price of college also entails ignoring a much simpler message about college costs which has proliferated throughout the media over the past several years: college tuition has soared over time, at a rate far greater than household income or inflation.

Enter the impulsive system, which anchors people's perceptions of what college would cost them not to the complicated personalized estimate they could obtain from an online net price calculator, but instead to what they hear on the news on an almost-daily basis: College tuition has skyrocketed. College is expensive. Therefore, we can't afford college. Not surprisingly, when researchers investigate families' perceptions of college costs, most people overestimate what college would cost their family. This pattern is particularly pronounced among students and parents from lower socioeconomic backgrounds (Avery & Kane, 2004; Grodsky & Jones, 2007; Horn, Chen, & Chapman, 2003).

## FACTORS AFFECTING OUR ABILITY
## TO NAVIGATE COMPLEX DECISIONS

This is not to say that our logical system does not push back against the simplifying strategies and conclusions from our impulsive system. Clearly, complex assignments get completed and well-informed decisions get made even in the face of complicated information. But engaging our analytic and deliberative processes requires a greater investment of cognitive energy. Certain factors increase the likelihood that we make this investment. For instance, many people buckle down and complete a challenging assignment when they are up against a deadline or because a sense of urgency prompts them to allocate more cognitive capacity to the task at hand. We're also more likely to invest cognitive attention when the consequences of the decision we are facing are both profound and immediate, such as evaluating different medical treatment options for someone.

At the same time, there are also factors that can decrease our ability to apply as much cognitive focus to complex decisions that we encounter. One of these factors is often within our control to influence, and that is the amount of external inputs that are competing for our attention. There's a reason that most people don't save their most complex tasks for when they're at home with kids running around, dinner to cook, and the radio on in the background. The more there is going on in our environments and competing for our attention, the less we are able to focus on a given task and the more likely our performance is to suffer (Karlan, McConnell, Mullainathan, & Zinman, 2010).

Texting while driving is a powerful illustration of how diverting our attention, in this case away from the road and to our phones, can have profound—and often disastrous—consequences. When people read and reply to texts while they are driving, it's not that they aren't paying *any* attention to the road. But the amount of attention they are focusing on driving is diminished now that they are applying some of their cognitive energy to processing the information in the text and thinking about something witty to say in response. Ninety-nine times out of a hundred, this decline in our attention doesn't end in disaster. But as the thousands of texting-related motor vehicle accidents each year demonstrate, even a small drop in our attention can negatively impact our reaction times and overall cognitive performance. Limiting the amount of environmental distractions often allows us to devote more of our cognitive resources to a task at hand—whether driving, working on a paper, or evaluating different school options we might be considering for our children.

Another factor impacting the amount of attention we have to devote to a task is the number and type of choices we encounter when making a decision. While this is not something we always can control, it is an aspect of the decision-making environment we encounter which can be readily influenced—whether by companies trying to sell us something or by educators or policy makers trying to promote high-quality schooling options. The idea of having more rather than fewer choices tends to be very popular among Americans. Many of us view the freedom to choose and the privilege of having a breadth of choices as integral components of the American political and free enterprise systems. Yet having a multitude of choices is not always conducive to making well-informed decisions—or, in some instances, any decision at all. When faced with many options, we have to exert greater cognitive energy in order to assess which choice best aligns with our preferences. Even with seemingly trivial choices, like deciding which jam to purchase in the supermarket, increasing the number of options people have to consider can substantially affect their decision-making ability.

To demonstrate how increasing the number of choices individuals encounter can influence the decisions they make, psychologists Sheena Iyengar and Mark Lepper (2000) conducted an experiment with supermarket jam offerings. Researchers dressed as store employees invited shoppers to sample a variety of Wilkin and Sons brand jams. The researchers randomly varied whether shoppers encountered twenty-four different jam varieties or just six jam varieties. An interesting pattern of responses occurred. On the one hand, shoppers who encountered the twenty-four jams were much more likely to stop at the booth than shoppers who encountered the six jams. Thus, the initial appeal of seeing many choices attracted more shoppers. On the other hand, shoppers who encountered the twenty-four jams were much less likely to actually purchase a jam: only 3 percent of shoppers who encountered the full range of jams actually purchased a jar, compared with 30 percent of the consumers who were faced with six choices. Thus, presenting people with a broad array of options can inhibit them from making any selection at all.

The consequences of choice complexity in decision making are often far more profound than whether shoppers purchase a Wilkin and Sons jam or not. And there need not be two dozen alternatives for the choices to introduce decision-making difficulty. As Donald Redelmeier and Eldar Shafir (1995) demonstrate, even highly educated physicians struggle to make decisions when presented with multiple alternatives. Redelmeier and Shafir sent family physicians in Canada letters describing a sixty-seven-year-old patient with osteoarthritis. At the end of the letter, half of the physicians were randomly selected to receive the following question about further treatment: "Before sending [the patient] away, however, you . . . find that there is one . . . medication that this patient has not tried (ibuprofen). What do you do?" Fifty-three percent of these physicians opted not to start a new medication and instead referred the patient for an orthopedic consult. The other half of physicians received the identical letter except for the final sentence: "Before sending [the patient] away, however, you . . . find that there are two . . . medications that this patient has not tried (ibuprofen and piroxicam). What do you do?" Just introducing one additional choice increased by 36 percent the probability that physicians opted not to start a new treatment in favor of an orthopedic referral. The added cognitive challenge of deciding between two options led more physicians to avoid making any choice at all, just as encountering twenty-four instead of six jam choices led fewer shoppers to purchase jams.

Choice complexity is affected not just by the number of choices but by the comparability between alternatives we encounter. Take, for example, choosing between Levi's 501 jeans and choosing between cold medicines (Lin, 2005). In the case of Levi's jeans, every pair looks the same (to me anyway); what varies are the dozens of different waist and length combinations. Here there are many choices, but the choices allow us to select the jeans that are the best fit for us individually. When we go shopping for cold remedies, on the other hand, every product is different, each offering its own combination of cures: some promise to soothe a cough and sore throat, some are for daytime and some for nighttime, and others promise to ease a cough and nasal congestion. Evaluating which particular cold remedy is right for us is much more difficult since the products differ on multiple dimensions. Just as limiting the amount of environmental distractions allows people to devote more cognitive focus to a task at hand, limiting the number of and/or simplifying the choices that people encounter can reduce the cognitive attention they have to allocate and increase the likelihood that they make active and informed decisions.

## DECISION MAKING AND ADOLESCENCE

Other factors that can negatively influence our ability to devote cognitive attention and energy to complex tasks are much less under our control. One is our age. While both the impulsive and logical systems are well developed by the time we reach adulthood, their development does not proceed at an equal rate. Recent neuroscientific research confirms what parents have long known about their teenagers: the parts of adolescents' brains which reply to immediate stimuli are firing on all cylinders, while the regions required for careful deliberation, thorough reasoning, and judgment are just coming off the assembly line (Casey, Jones, & Somerville, 2011; Steinberg, 2008; Steinberg, Cauffman, Woolard, Graham, & Banich, 2009). For the average teenager, the more onerous responsibilities of tomorrow seem infinitely far away compared with the pleasures and opportunities of today. This helps explain why so many high school and college students wind up pulling all-nighters to complete final papers or projects. When it comes down to a choice between working on a paper a couple weeks before it's due and (1) going out with friends, (2) being on Instagram, (3) watching TV, or (4) all of the above, working on the paper typically doesn't have much of a fighting chance.

The differential development of the impulsive and deliberative systems within adolescents' brains also helps explain the rise of the helicopter parent phenomenon. Parents—particularly those who went to college themselves—are keenly aware of the importance of having a college degree in today's economy and, even more so, attentive to opportunities that attending a selective college or university can create for their child. This awareness, in turn, prompts parents to focus considerable attention on the tasks their child must complete in order to access one of these colleges: taking (and in many cases retaking) college entrance exams, visiting colleges, drafting essays and obtaining recommendation letters, and completing all the application and financial aid paperwork that colleges typically require.

Most adolescents aspire to go to college and in a general way recognize the importance of a college degree to their future success (Avery & Kane, 2004). Yet a vague recognition of the benefits of college—especially when those benefits accrue many years in the future—is often not sufficient to catalyze independent action to complete application-related tasks. After all, many of these tasks require strong organizational, planning, and reasoning skills that are often still in the developmental phase among adolescents (Keating, 2004). And any inclination teenagers might feel to focus on these onerous tasks has to compete against strong biological impulses toward more immediate and enjoyable pursuits. As a result, a common battle is waged in households across America:

PARENT: Have you started your college essay yet? The Common Application is due in 10 days!

TEENAGER: I'm still thinking of ideas. But I'm busy right now.

PARENT: You need to work on this now! Didn't we talk about leaving enough time so that your English teacher and Mr. Hernandez—who went to Harvard, remember—have time to read your essay and give you feedback?

TEENAGER: Stop interrupting me! I'm talking to my friends.

PARENT: I don't hear you talking to anyone.

TEENAGER: On Snapchat!

PARENTS: Well, tell your Snapchat friends you have five more minutes before you're logging off and working on your essay.

Much as teenagers resent this intrusion in the moment, they also benefit from their parents' ability to keep track of deadlines, organize and set intermediate steps that build toward completion of a complex task, and emphasize doing a task in the moment rather than continuing to put it off. In more affluent communities, school-based college counselors and private college planning consultants offer additional support for college-bound teens by helping them manage the complex work of applying.

## DECISION MAKING AND SCARCITY

Each of these factors influencing our decision making—environmental distractions, choice complexity, adolescent cognitive development—involves a form of scarcity. The more distractions we encounter, the less attention we can devote to a task at hand. When we confront choices that are too numerous or complex, we may lack the cognitive resources necessary to make a decision. Teenagers, given their stage of cognitive development, experience scarcity of a different sort: neurological capacity for long-term planning, organization, and judgment. Behavioral economists Sendhil Mullainathan and Eldar Shafir (2013), authors of the aptly titled *Scarcity*, illustrate the many ways in which scarcity of one form or another negatively influences our cognitive performance and our ability to make well-informed and well-reasoned decisions. Even something as simple as background noise creates a scarcity of concentration which can have detrimental effects. Mullainathan and Shafir describe a school in New Haven, Connecticut, where one sixth-grade class was on the side of a building facing railroad tracks where trains rumbled by multiple times during the day, while the other sixth-grade class was on the opposite side of the building. Students on the train side performed a full grade level below their counterparts on the quiet side of the building. When the city soundproofed the train-side classroom, performance differences disappeared.

Poverty is perhaps the most challenging and pernicious form of scarcity individuals face, and as Mullainathan and Shafir show, impoverishment can have a profound influence on our cognitive performance and decision making. To illustrate the relationship between financial scarcity and cognitive performance, the authors, along with Jiaying Zhao, presented the following scenario to people in a New Jersey mall: "Imagine that your car has some trouble, which requires a $300 service. Your auto insurance will cover half the cost. You need to decide whether to go ahead and get the car fixed, or take a chance and hope that it lasts for a while longer. How would you go about making such a decision? Financially, would it be an easy or a difficult decision for you to make?"

After posing this question, the researchers administered a cognitive assessment to participants. Drawing on self-reported household income information that participants provided at the start of the study, Mullainathan, Shafir, and Zhao found that wealthier and lower-income people performed equally following this prompt. The authors then presented a slightly different scenario to a second group of mall visitors: "Imagine that your car has some trouble, which requires a $3,000 service. Your auto insurance will cover half the cost. You need to decide whether to go ahead and get the car fixed, or take a chance and hope that it lasts for a while longer. How would you go about making such a decision? Financially, would it be an easy or a difficult decision for you to make?"

Once again, the researchers administered a cognitive assessment following this prompt. The wealthy respondents performed just as high as their counterparts in the first scenario—whether the repair bill was $300 or $3,000 would not materially affect their financial well-being, and so the cognitive capacity they were able to dedicate to the intelligence test was unaffected. For the lower-income respondents, however, the idea of a $3,000 bill triggered broader financial anxieties. A substantial portion of their cognitive capacity was now preoccupied with monetary concerns, and as a result their performance on the assessment suffered.

The results from this experiment reiterate an important point: decision-making challenges that youths and families from disadvantaged backgrounds encounter are not emblematic of lower underlying intelligence or ability. As Mullainathan, Shafir, and Zhao found, rich and poor participants performed equally well when the repair bill was modest. When confronted with a source of financial stress, however, lower-income participants had diminished cognitive capacity to devote to the assessment. They were just as intelligent and capable, but in the presence of monetary concerns they were less able to exercise their full cognitive abilities.

The authors' findings bear out in a variety of settings. One of the most intriguing studies involved sugar cane farmers in India. Like most crops, sugar cane is harvested all at once and growers paid in one lump sum, meaning that farmers have a substantial influx of cash right after harvesting but are often quite cash strapped leading up to the harvest. Prior to harvesting, they are not so resource poor that their food intake drops, but they do have less discretionary funds to spend on other consumer goods. In other words, the sugar cane farmers face substantially greater scarcity in the months preceding the harvest than they do in the months following the harvest. Once again the authors administered a cognitive assessment to farmers a few weeks before the harvest, when they had little cash but before they had to exert physical effort on harvesting sugar cane, and again after the harvest, when they had substantial cash. Farmers consistently scored substantially higher on the cognitive assessment following the cash influx. By alleviating the relative economic poverty farmers had experienced, the sugar cane crop payment increased the cognitive energy and attention they could devote to other tasks.

In sum, navigating complex decisions requires an investment of substantial cognitive energy and attention. Making this investment is more challenging when we are faced with external distractions or many choices, particularly so for adolescents and people experiencing poverty and other forms of scarcity. With cognitive capacity pushed to the limit (or over the limit), it's common for people to put off making a decision, not make any decision at all, or use a simplifying strategy to inform their choice which may not lead them to an outcome that aligns well with their priorities and intentions.

### SUPPORTING DECISION MAKING IN THE FACE OF COMPLEXITY

Fortunately, researchers have developed a range of behavioral solutions that address informational complexity and support people in making more informed decisions. One set of approaches aims to directly reduce complexity by simplifying information that people have to consider when making a choice. A different strategy stems from the recognition that in the face of complexity, many people simply don't make any decision at all, as with the jam study described above. In numerous instances, failing to make an active decision means that people wind up with whatever the default is. For example, in some companies employees have to opt in to participate in an employer-sponsored retirement program. Yet participating in the program often requires people to evaluate a complicated array of investment options and select the one to which their funds will be directed. Faced with this complexity, many people do not choose any investment at all and leave the retirement program—and the employer match that comes with it—on the table. Researchers have found that changing the default condition so that employees are automatically enrolled in a retirement program unless they actively choose not to participate substantially boosts participation rates.

Another set of efforts aims to reduce hassles associated with decisions or offer assistance in navigating complex processes. This can take the form of simplifying an application for people to participate in a government-sponsored program, or making it easy for people to connect with professional advisors when faced with a challenging decision. Reducing hassles is a strategy that the corporate sector has long recognized as good for business. For instance, think of the number of websites (Amazon, Fidelity, Verizon, Nike) that now offer live chat assistance. Rather than having to slog through a customer service phone line or wait for an e-mail response, help with all of our shopping needs is now just a click away!

A different approach focuses on how information is framed. For instance, emphasizing the immediacy of a deadline or a potential loss people may face by not taking action can motivate people to make a decision. A related set of strategies aims to help people follow through on intentions they have established for themselves. For instance, providing people with personalized reminders of tasks they need to complete in order to achieve a goal can help them maintain attention. Similarly, providing people with a prompt to plan out when important tasks will get done can help them translate their intentions into action. Finally, giving people a way to commit to following through on an intended action can help them realize their goal even in the face of near-term distractions.

It is worth noting that many of these strategies build on each other. For instance, sending people reminders of tasks they need to complete in order to achieve a goal often involves providing them with simplified information related to that goal. As I describe these strategies in greater depth in the following chapters, I primarily focus on one strategy (or set of strategies) at a time for the sake of explanation and clarity. But there are clearly instances when these strategies are tightly interwoven.

In the remainder of this chapter I focus on direct simplification of information as a strategy to reduce complexity and guide people toward more informed decision making. In subsequent chapters I explore in detail the other behavioral strategies to overcome complexity.

## POLICY INTERVENTIONS TO SIMPLIFY INFORMATION

As with jam purchases or medical diagnoses, the logic behind information simplification as a policy strategy to help people make more informed decisions is straightforward: by reducing the complexity or sheer amount of information that people need to process, they are more likely to invest cognitive energy and attention in the decision-making process. This enables their logical neurological system to kick into gear and enhances the probability that they will make a choice well suited to their priorities.

Two pioneering studies that used information simplification to support more informed decision making were in the fields of retirement planning and health care. As I mention briefly above (and discuss in more detail in the next chapter), early behavioral work to address complexity came in the form of changing defaults for whether people had to opt into or opt out of an employer-sponsored retirement program. In a related line of work, John Beshears and colleagues (2012) investigated the impact of companies providing simplified enrollment strategies for retirement programs. Employees still had to opt into the program, but they were offered a Quick Enrollment option through which they could check one box and participate at an asset allocation and contribution rate preselected by the employer. The Quick Enrollment strategy eliminated the complexity of employees having to evaluate and choose from hundreds of investment options and simplified the decision employees faced to a Yes/No choice: participate in the preselected retirement program or not.[2] This decision required substantially less cognitive processing, and not surprisingly, many more employees made active choices about whether to participate. Within one company that adopted the Quick Enrollment strategy, retirement program participation rates tripled among new hires compared with those before Quick Enrollment was offered. Among existing employees at the company who had not participated in the retirement program, 25 percent opted to join the program when offered Quick Enrollment.

A similar approach was taken to help senior citizens evaluate which Medicare Part D prescription drug benefit plan to enroll in. Under Medicare Part D, seniors could choose among 40–60 different drug coverage plans, depending on where they lived. Jeffrey Kling and coauthors (2012) investigated the effect of proactively sending seniors personalized and simplified information about how the costs of their drug regimen would vary across different plans. Targeting seniors who were enrolled in a current drug plan, the authors sent a randomly selected group personalized letters that indicated, in a simple table, their current plan, what this plan would cost in the following year, the lowest-cost plan available to them in the following year, and what they would save by switching to the other plan. The control group received a letter that provided a website address where seniors could obtain the same information themselves. The distinction here is important: *all* seniors had easy access to the same personalized and simplified information about the drug coverage plan that would yield the greatest cost savings. The key difference was that the first group had this information actively delivered to them, whereas the second group would have to seek this information out themselves. The authors found that the prompt to access simplified information about costs associated with drug plans was impactful for both groups, but particularly so for the group that received personalized information in their letters. Twenty-eight percent of these seniors changed plans, compared with 17 percent of seniors who were directed to the website. The intervention generated approximately $100 in cost savings per senior, per year.

Both of these studies demonstrate that reducing the complexity of information about available options can substantially increase the probability that people make active choices, and that these active choices often lead them to better outcomes.

## INFORMATIONAL COMPLEXITY IN EDUCATION

The education sector is rife with examples of complex information that students and families must access and decipher to gain a full sense of their schooling options. Many communities have school choice programs, for example, that are designed to allow students and parents to identify elementary, middle, or high schools that meet important considerations for the family: academic quality, but also sports offered, geographic location, transportation accessibility, and other criteria. The challenge is that providing this information for the dozens or even hundreds of schools that are open to families can require dense booklets that are often in excess of a hundred pages. Presented with such detailed information and given what we know about how people respond in the face of complexity, it is not surprising that parents sometimes opt to keep their child in the residentially zoned school even when higher-quality options are available.

The college search process requires students and parents to digest an even more complicated array of information about available postsecondary options. Colleges vary considerably in their quality, affordability, and academic and extracurricular options. On the one hand, extensive choice means that students have a better chance of finding a school that has quality academic programs in a field they are interested in pursuing and that is within their family's budget. On the other hand, there are thousands of colleges across the country, so finding a school that is well matched (broadly speaking) for each student is far from straightforward. There are any number of online college search engines that, in theory, should help facilitate the process of students finding colleges that are a good fit for their interests and abilities, but in practice this is cognitively a very demanding task. Choosing between colleges is particularly daunting because they differ on so many dimensions. Some campuses are in urban settings, while others are more rural; some institutions have heavily proscribed course sequences, while others allow students much more curricular flexibility. These many differences between colleges and universities make it that much harder for families to thoroughly compare institutions and identify the set that are best suited for the student's abilities and interests.

As a result, students often use simplifying strategies to decide which colleges to attend: the college that is closest to home; the college where the student felt a strong connection with their tour guide; the college with the nicest dorm rooms or dining facilities. Unfortunately, the ways that students and their families simplify the college choice do not always directly relate to factors that contribute to their potential success (or failure) at the institution, such as the quality of instruction and advising or the job market placements of graduates.

And as challenging as it is for families to make well-informed decisions about picking a college, parents of preschool-age children face an arguably even greater decision-making hurdle.[3] For one thing, parents have to wade through a set of complicated eligibility criteria to determine whether their child is even qualified to participate in a given early childhood learning program. These eligibility criteria often vary from the federal Head Start program to state-sponsored early childhood centers and state- or community-based child care subsidy programs. In some communities, pressing considerations such as hours of operation and proximity to work may preclude families from choosing centers based on the quality of care provided to their children. Finally, while information about school quality is frequently available to parents of school- and college-age children, in many communities information about early childhood center quality is quite limited.

As more states adopt Quality Ratings Information Systems (QRIS) for early childhood centers, this is starting to change.[4] But QRIS are in the early stage of development. In many states it is still optional for centers to participate, which may preclude parents from accessing quality measures about all day care options they are considering. Another challenge is that QRIS are not always very helpful at differentiating high-quality from low-quality centers. In Minnesota and Tennessee, for instance, 75 percent of centers are rated as high quality by the state QRIS (Tout et al., 2010). Unfortunately, while most states with QRIS make this information available online, so far few states have undertaken proactive campaigns to bring this information directly into the hands (or computers and mobile devices) of parents, particularly those in economically disadvantaged communities, whose children stand to benefit the most from quality care.

A final challenge with QRIS relates to the scarcity issue I describe above, and it is one to which I can very much relate as the father of two young children. Balancing the competing demands of work and caring for two young children requires a tremendous investment of energy and often is accompanied by sleep deprivation over an extended time period (in the case of my daughter, five-plus years before she slept through the night). As a result, even parents who access the QRIS data may struggle to make informed child care decisions. The cognitive bandwidth they can allocate to deciphering QRIS information may be quite diminished because of the energy and attention they are expending on their children and work responsibilities. This cognitive distraction, as we have seen, is compounded in economically challenged families.

## INFORMATION SIMPLIFICATION TO
## IMPROVE EDUCATIONAL OUTCOMES

Just as providing people with simplified information has led to improved outcomes in the retirement planning and health coverage sectors, several interventions have demonstrated that providing students and families with simplified information about school choices can lead to higher-quality enrollments. One of the pioneering studies in this arena was conducted by

Justine Hastings and Michael Weinstein (2008) in the Charlotte-Mecklenburg Public Schools (CMS) in North Carolina. In 2002, parents of CMS students were able to submit their top three choices for their child's school placement. However, evaluating school options required parents to refer to a school choice guide that was more than a hundred pages long and contained each school's self-assessment of the positive attributes of their school. This guide did not contain objective measures of each school's test performance. Parents who wanted to consider test scores to get some measure of school quality had to visit the CMS website and look up each school's performance one at a time. Perhaps as a result of this complexity—and, for some families, satisfaction with their local school—only 11 percent of parents submitted forms requesting a change to their child's assigned school.

In 2004, CMS implemented a change to this policy. With the onset of No Child Left Behind regulations, the district was now required to provide parents in underperforming schools with additional information about test scores at all district schools. Included with the school choice forms that the district sent to parents was a three-page spreadsheet that showed each school's test score. Just as the Quick Enrollment program reduced the retirement decision employees faced to a simple "Yes, enroll" or "No, do not enroll" consideration, this shift in CMS school choice information substantially reduced the amount of information parents had to process when evaluating schooling options for their child. They no longer had to wade through over a hundred pages of schools' narrative self-assessments; now, parents could compare schools on a common and singular (if imperfect) measure of school quality.

This straightforward shift in the school choice information provided by CMS increased the share of parents who actively selected a school other than their guaranteed option by five to seven percentage points and increased the average test scores of the schools their children attended. Attending a higher-scoring school, in turn, had a positive effect on students, raising their own scores by a substantial margin. Interestingly, one of the primary predictors of whether families chose an alternative school was whether they had a higher-scoring option within close proximity to where they lived. This suggests that information simplification is particularly impactful on school decision making when other costs associated with switching schools, such as travel time and expense, are lower.

Jon Valant and Susanna Loeb conducted a similar experiment in Milwaukee, Wisconsin, and Washington, DC (Valant, 2014). As in CMS, both districts have active school choice programs. Families in Milwaukee can also request up to three school choices, while in Washington families can request one of the district's specialized schools or up to six schools outside of their neighborhood-assigned school. Unlike in CMS, however, the districts did not actively disseminate information about school choice at the time of Valant and Loeb's experiment. Rather, families interested in learning about school choices would have to seek out information about school options on the district's websites, request printed information from their current school or from the district office, or seek out information from other sources.

During the 2010–2011 academic year, the authors collaborated with the nonprofit organization GreatSchools to distribute school choice booklets to families in both Milwaukee and Washington. At first glance the booklets appeared to go the opposite direction of CMS's school choice simplification efforts. The GreatSchools booklets were 144 and 170 pages long in Milwaukee and Washington, respectively. Rather than provide families with narrative self-assessments from each school, however, GreatSchools designed the booklet content to capitalize on people's tendency to use simplifying strategies in the face of complex information. In both cities, each school's profile included basic information such as the location, grade levels offered, and which extracurricular programs were offered. In Milwaukee, this information was accompanied by a chart indicating a school's math and reading performance, with the strongest scores marked with a green traffic light. In Washington, the school information was accompanied by a five-star rating system, with high-performing schools receiving five stars and lower-performing schools receiving fewer stars.

Like the Quick Enrollment and the CMS interventions, this approach allowed students and parents to simplify their school choice decisions to a single, comparable dimension. But the GreatSchools approach went a step further in its attempt at simplification. The visual cue of a green light or five stars made it that much easier for families to identify schools with stronger performance. Families still had the option of reading more detailed information about each school, but the visual cues provided a quick and easy way for parents to zero in on higher-performing options.

To investigate the impact of the GreatSchools school choice information on families' school choices, Valant and Loeb randomly selected which schools in each district would receive the booklets. As with the Hastings and Weinstein study, the authors found that disseminating the Great-Schools booklets led parents to enroll their elementary school children in more highly rated middle schools, measured either by schools' average performance on standardized tests or by GreatSchools' stoplight and star rating systems. Interestingly, however, middle school students in schools that received GreatSchools booklets enrolled in high schools with significantly *lower* average academic performance.

In both cases the provision of simplified information had a substantial influence on families' school choices. But the negative effects on the academic quality attended by middle schoolers raise an important cautionary note about strategies to simplify information: recipients do not always respond to information in the way that educators or policy makers intend. In the case of the GreatSchools study, the authors interpret the negative effects for middle schoolers as a function of students taking a more active role in choosing a school. While the authors do not have evidence of what particular aspect of the booklets would lead middle schoolers to enroll at lower-quality schools, one hypothesis is that students were intimidated by the prospect of attending the most highly rated schools, which they may have perceived to be overly challenging. I will return to this interesting question of the potential unintended consequences of behavioral interventions in the conclusion.

Choosing well-matched colleges similarly requires that families navigate highly complex information. There are various indications that this complexity may deter academically accomplished, low-income students from picking institutions that are well matched to their abilities and from which they have a greater chance of graduating. As many as half of lower-socioeconomic-status students don't even apply to selective colleges they would be eligible to attend (Bowen, Chingos, & McPherson, 2009; Hoxby & Avery, 2012; Smith, Pender, & Howell, 2013). Among the highest-achieving students, only 34 percent of low-income students attend one of the most selective colleges and universities in the country, compared with 78 percent of upper-income students (Hoxby & Avery, 2012).

An entire industry has cropped up to simplify the college search process and assist students in attending better-matched institutions: in addition to private admissions counselors available to more affluent families, there are online search engines and mobile apps that provide customized guidance and reminders about key stages in the application process. Both state and federal governments have invested substantially in online tools to simplify college search. For instance, in 2013 the White House and the Department of Education launched the College Scorecard, which provides a graphic interface through which students can identify criteria that are important to their college selection, such as location, size, and academic programs offered. After students have selected the factors that are most important to them, the Scorecard presents them with clever graphics to highlight important dimensions about each institution: a fuel-gauge-like indicator illustrating how the college's net costs compare with those of other institutions, and a thermometer-type scale showing how the institutions' graduation rate stacks up to the nationwide average. These easy-to-digest graphics of college information have the potential to substantially simplify the search process for students and families.

For online college search tools like the Scorecard to be successful, however, people need to know they exist. Yet many of the college search engines are designed with the same "if we build it, they will come" mentality that characterizes most of the QRIS in early childhood education. The developers of these search tools focus more on the effective interface than on promoting their use. Many high-quality resources go unused because target populations, particularly students and parents from economically disadvantaged backgrounds, are unaware of their existence. Further, many struggle to understand how to make effective use of these tools. One obvious distribution channel for this type of information would be students' high schools. In many communities, however, the school counselor–to–student ratio is 500:1, and counselors typically spend 20 percent of their time or less on college planning and applications (Civic Enterprises, 2011). As a result, the panoply of online and mobile tools that were designed to streamline the college search process are not reaching many of the families who would benefit most from this simplified information.

Caroline Hoxby and Sarah Turner (2013) developed an innovative solution to this information problem. In collaboration with the College Board, Hoxby and Turner identified low-income high school seniors across the country who had scored in the top 10 percent of SAT takers nationwide. The authors sent these students customized packets of college and financial aid information to help guide their search. The packets identified selective colleges to which the student had a good chance of being admitted based on their SAT scores. For each institution, the authors included information on institutional quality, such as the average six-year graduation rate, and estimates of how much each school would cost. It also calculated the total amount of federal, state, and institutional financial aid the student was likely to receive. Hoxby and Turner also included the same information for randomly drawn community colleges and four-year institutions in each student's state so they could see how the quality and affordability of more selective institutions compared with those of their other postsecondary options. Finally, the packets included application fee waivers so that up-front costs would not deter students from applying to well-matched institutions.

The packets cost just $6 to distribute to students and their families, yet they had a pronounced effect on students' application and enrollment patterns. Students were substantially more likely to attend colleges with higher graduation rates, with academically stronger peers (measured by the median SAT score of students at the institution), and that invested more instructional dollars per student.

## ADDITIONAL OPPORTUNITIES TO SIMPLIFY
## INFORMATION IN EDUCATION

There are lots of opportunities to apply this idea to students at all levels in an effort to help them make better educational choices. Early on, there is clearly room to provide parents with more information about child care center and preschool quality, which should be increasingly possible as states expand their QRIS. Some communities are starting to require early childhood education centers to post their QRIS rating at the entrance so that parents have easy access to straightforward information about the center's quality. Much like the CMS, Milwaukee, and Washington, DC, school choice studies, we can improve the design and distribution of QRIS information to families who are unlikely to see this information online. In chapter 3, we'll look at how the way information is *delivered* can affect decision making.

At the high school level, one approach gaining momentum is to use predictive analytics to identify whether students' performance is preparing them for success in higher education. With funding from the Bill and Melinda Gates Foundation, several school districts across the country have partnered with researchers to develop college readiness indicators. These systems track a variety of measures—including student course performance, but also measures such as academic tenacity and college knowledge—in order to assess each student's readiness for college. While these indicators have been directed toward guiding teachers, they could also be adapted to provide families with useful information about their child's progress.

Information simplification efforts shouldn't be limited to students and families. Many communities are trying to develop better systems for measuring teacher effectiveness, particularly in light of research showing that high-quality teachers have a profound impact on their students' lifelong achievement (Chetty, Friedman, and Rockoff, 2011). Principals and superintendents, however, are faced with a complicated array of ways to evaluate their teachers: observations, improvements in student test scores, student and/or parent evaluations, and teacher self-evaluations. Several recent studies have investigated the impact of providing school leaders with more simplified information about teacher performance. In one study, for instance, school principals in New York City received reports on how far individual teachers had raised their students' scores in math and English (Rockoff, Staiger, Kane, & Taylor, 2010). This information was meant not to replace evaluative information the principals were already gathering (for example, classroom observations of the teacher's performance), but to supplement it. The authors of the study found that in schools whose principals received the information about teacher performance, lower-performing teachers were more likely to leave and student achievement modestly improved.

In higher education, one obvious place we could simplify information is around financial aid, specifically student loans. Students are borrowing more to finance their education, while default rates have nearly doubled over the past decade. Borrowers face profound consequences from overborrowing and defaulting, including long-term indebtedness, garnished wages, and little chance for future financial aid. From the moment students first explore their borrowing options to when they enter into loan repayment, they encounter a staggeringly complex array of information and choices. This may lead to students borrowing more than they can ever hope to repay. Students often don't know they have the freedom to choose how much to borrow and do not have to accept the maximum amount of loans offered by a lender. They may be unaware of the various repayment options available to them or how the repayment option impacts how much they will owe in monthly payments. Students can be daunted by the challenge of weighing the potential returns of different degree programs against the loans they would need to take to pursue those programs. At an even more basic level, students—particularly those who take time off during their education or who attend multiple institutions—may have a hard time keeping track of how much they have borrowed over time.

Indiana University recently launched an initiative to provide potential loan borrowers with simplified information about how much they had currently borrowed and what they already owed in monthly payments based on their debt (Lorin, 2014). Starting in the 2012–2013 academic year, the university sent students a simple, personalized letter that reported this information and identified campus-based financial planning resources students could access to make informed choices for the coming year. The university credits these letters with generating a $31 million drop in the amount of federal loans students assumed for the 2013–2013 academic year.[5]

Several broad principles underlie these efforts to help families make better choices about their educational options:

1. Identify complex and hard-to-compare information about the wide variety of choices and options.
2. Simplify this information in a way that reduces the complexity of the decision and provides students and families with strategies (like visual cues or reference points) to guide their decision making.
3. Proactively deliver this information to families rather than relying on them to find it for themselves.

A fourth principle that I have not discussed as much in this chapter but consider carefully in the conclusion is to think carefully about the unintended consequences of our information simplification efforts. While people are more likely to make a decision when presented with simplified information, this does not necessarily mean that they will make decisions in the way that we expect them to. This is particularly a concern if, by virtue of simplifying information, we lead people to make choices that result in outcomes in which they are worse off. One way to prevent this is to *test* any information simplification effort with a broad range of constituents—including students and families—before distributing this information more broadly.

In the chapters that follow, we'll look at how the way information is framed and delivered can have a substantial influence on the decisions people make. But first, I turn to the importance of considering the status quo: the educational experiences students overwhelmed with choices encounter if they fail to make any decision at all.

# Chapter 2

. . . . . . . . . . . . . . .

# Starting with the Status Quo

ONE OF MY ALL-TIME FAVORITE television shows is the American version of The Office. And, my favorite Office episode is undoubtedly "Scott's Tots." The episode (in the show's sixth season) opens with Erin, the office receptionist, entering the staff break room to ask Pam (formerly the receptionist and now a member of the Dunder Mifflin sales staff) to review the day's itinerary for Michael Scott, the Dunder Mifflin regional manager. Pam looks over the itinerary and asks, "What's 'Scott's Tots'?" Stanley, another member of the staff, is reading a newspaper and erupts in laughter at Pam's question. When he can finally contain himself, he asks, "Has it really been ten years?" The camera cuts to Stanley holding up a decade-old newspaper article with the headline, "Local Businessman Pledges College Tuition to Third Graders." Michael, with all the best intentions but no financial resources to support his promise, had made this pledge to a local elementary school classroom ten years before—and had never quite managed to extricate himself from the commitment.

Pam, in alarm, asks Michael why he would make that promise to young kids. "To change lives," Michael responded. Pam tells Michael what a terrible thing he had done, and he asks Erin to call the school to postpone the visit. Erin reminds Michael that he's already postponed six times. Fast-forward several minutes in the episode, and Michael and Erin arrive at the school. They are greeted by wildly cheering teenagers who are now seniors in high school and all planning to go on to college. They are wearing T-shirts with "Scott's Tots" written across the front. Michael is given the seat of honor at the front of the classroom. The principal stands up and says, "Scott's Tots, who are ready to graduate, thought it was time to give you a proper thank-you." The students break out into song and dance, chanting, "Hey Mr. Scott, watcha gonna do, watcha gonna do, make our dreams come true?" This may be one of the most intentionally awkward moments in television history.

Needless to say, the students are shocked, disappointed, and angry when Michael finally tells them he doesn't have the money to pay for their college educations. He is booed out of the room and about to get in his car when a student confronts him. The student tells him that making a promise he couldn't keep was wrong. Michael, clearly wracked with guilt, offers to pay for the student's college books and gives him a set of checks to cash over the next four years.

On the car ride back to the office, Michael is devastated. "Fifteen lives," he moans. "I destroyed fifteen young lives today." Erin, attempting to console him, first tells Michael that there's financial aid the students could receive, or maybe they could join the Army or Navy. She then adds, "The principal told me that 90 percent of Scott's Tots are on track to graduate, and that's 35 percent higher than the rest of the school's [graduation rate]. I think if you hadn't made that promise, a lot of them would have dropped out, which is something to think about . . . I think."

Erin's comment reveals the power that the status quo has to influence our decisions. Implicit in her reasoning is the idea that when Michael promised a class of third graders to pay for their college tuition, he profoundly changed their view of future possibilities. Many of these kids may have been from families where few adults had gone to college and in which a substantial share of young people dropped out before graduation. Absent Michael's promise, these children would have grown up—like their peers—with the idea that going to college was the exception to the rule, an unlikely course for their lives. Michael's commitment disrupted the view of what was possible. Now, in their minds, college was paid for. For these third graders, not only did Michael believe they could succeed in college, but he was going to eliminate a major obstacle blocking their success. All they had to do was stay in school, work hard, and graduate. Boneheaded and empty as Michael's promise turned out to be, there's probably truth in Erin's assessment that it changed the educational trajectory of these kids.

## THE SUBTLE POWER OF THE STATUS QUO

Deciphering complex information about choices we are presented with, or choosing between these choices, requires a substantial investment of cognitive energy. A common response for many people in the face of informational and choice complexity is to put off making a decision or, worse, to be completely paralyzed by it. Confronted with hard choices, we don't choose and then automatically revert to the status quo—the default or way things are. Researchers James J. Choi, David Laibson, Brigitte Madrian, and Andrew Metrick (2003), who have studied the power of the status quo extensively in the context of retirement planning, refer to this as "passive decision-making."

Not every complex decision has a clear status quo. In some cases, people are very aware of the outcomes from failing to make a decision. Take, for instance, income tax. Preparing and paying our taxes has to rank high on the list of Americans' most unpleasant tasks of the year. Tax preparation requires gathering a bunch of paperwork, answering an extensive set of complicated questions, and, worst of all, often parting with hard-earned money. It's not surprising, then, that many people—yours truly included—put off preparing their taxes until the last possible minute. But at the end of the day, most people do prepare and pay their taxes. Failing to take any action at all would result in even more unpleasant outcomes—penalties and legal action from the IRS—that are sufficiently painful that most of us complete our taxes before the deadline.

There are many other decisions, however, where the consequence (either positive or negative) of failing to make a decision is either too trivial, too far in the future, or too unlikely to serve as compelling motivation. Before sitting down to write this morning, I looked for the fiftieth time at an e-mail sitting in my inbox from a local farm that runs a community-supported agriculture program. For a $250 seasonal share we'd get a big bag of locally grown produce every week for ten weeks. My family eats a lot of vegetables—we spend at least $25 on vegetables at the supermarket every week—and I like the idea of supporting a local farm. But I have to print out this form, decide whether I want to pay the $250 up front or in separate payments, find my checkbook, write a check, and remember to put it in the mail (can you guess why just about everyone has moved to online order forms?). If I don't do anything, it's not like we're going to starve. I'll still get vegetables from the store, albeit less fresh and tasty, but the consequence of not making a decision is pretty insignificant. In cases such as these, even these tiny hurdles can prevent people from following through on their intentions and instead lead to them sticking with the status quo.

Even with seemingly trivial decisions, however, the course of action we pursue can be substantially influenced by subtle changes in the status quo. Kareem Haggag and Giovanni Paci (2014) examined, for instance, how changes in the default tip amounts that New York City taxicab riders are encouraged to provide influence how much they give. The authors capitalize on an idiosyncratic rule by one of the companies that operates the credit card machines in taxicabs to investigate the effect of defaults on low-stakes choices. For passengers whose fare was under $15, the payment touch screen invited riders to enter in their own tip amount or choose from three preselected amounts: $2, $3, and $4. For passengers whose fare was over $15, the structure of choices was the same, but instead of dollar amounts for the tip, riders were presented with both percentage tips (20 percent, 25 percent, and 30 percent) and the corresponding dollar amounts. For example, a 20 percent tip on a $15 cab ride would be $3. This subtle change meant that people with nearly identical fares (for instance, $14.99 and $15.00) were presented with suggested tip amounts that varied by as much as a dollar—in other words, the person with a $14.99 fare saw $2, $3, and $4 options, while the person with the $15 fare saw 20 percent, 25 percent, and 30 percent. So if the rider was inclined to choose the smallest option, the difference of a penny in the fare would result in a difference of $1 in the tip. If people have strong views about how much to tip for a given cab fare and ride experience, this difference shouldn't affect how much they tip. After all, passengers were still free to enter their own tip amount. The authors found, however, that the subtle prompt to contribute more, in the form of percentages over the fare, increased tip amounts by over 10 percent. I travel quite often, and even having read these papers, I find myself opting for the preselected percentage tip buttons, even when it leads me to pay a higher tip than I would otherwise be inclined to offer.

While people are rarely aware of it, we increasingly encounter similar efforts to shift defaults in ways that influence our spending decisions. The Chili's restaurant company, for instance, recently began installing smart tablets on all its tables so that diners can order and pay for their dinners directly, without having to interact with a server (Garber, 2014). Like in the taxicabs, diners are now presented with the default option of giving servers a 20 percent tip. These same tablets prompt our eating habits in ways we are rarely conscious of—an idea I return to in the next chapter.

Retirement investments are another example of a decision that has substantial financial consequences. The benefits, however, may appear too far into the future to catalyze many of us to invest the energy and attention necessary to evaluate and act on our options. Economist Brigitte Madrian and colleague Dennis Shea (2001) studied how default conditions can affect retirement decisions at a Fortune 500 health care company. Prior to April 1, 1998, employees had to actively elect to participate in the company's retirement program. Those who did could contribute anywhere from 1 to 15 percent of their salaries to the company's 401(k) plan, with the employer making a matching contribution of up to 3 percent of the employee's salary. Employees had to overcome several cognitive hurdles in order to participate in the program. The first, and perhaps most straightforward, was to allocate time to actually complete the necessary forms. Employees then had to choose how much of their salary to invest in the 401(k) plan and—even more challenging—how to distribute this investment across the many available investment options.

Not surprisingly, given this complexity, fewer than half of employees who had been hired just before the policy change had enrolled in the retirement plan. This raises an interesting distinction about the types of decisions for which people are likely to passively opt for the status quo—in this case, not participating in the retirement program. On the one hand, the consequences of not making an active decision are quite substantial—employees forego not only the employer match to their contribution but also the advantages of contributing pretax dollars toward retirement savings. Yet for many new employees, retirement is decades away, and the potential financial returns of retirement investments are little more than numbers on a spreadsheet. As employees aged, however, retirement savings became more salient. Interestingly, Madrian and Shea found that when employees had to opt in to the retirement plan, participation rates in the plan increased along with employees' tenure with the company. While fewer than half of employees hired just before the policy change participated in the retirement program, 80 percent of employees who had been with the company for ten to fifteen years participated. This increase in participation rate may have reflected both employees' increasing financial literacy and their ability to more efficiently evaluate the various investment options, but also the growing understanding of the importance of contributing toward their retirement.

Changing the enrollment policy so that employees were defaulted into the retirement program unless they actively opted not to participate did not change any of the key financial terms. But by eliminating the complex decisions that employees had to make in order to participate when it was an opt-in program, this policy shift had a dramatic effect on participation rates. Eighty-six percent of new employees participated in the company's retirement program—this was 3 percent higher than the participation rate among employees who had been with the company for over twenty years! As a further illustration of the power of changing the status quo, not only were employees more likely to participate in the program, but they were also substantially more likely to stay with the contribution rate and fund allocation set as a default (Madrian & Shea, 2001).

Defaults are also quite powerful when the outcomes of our decisions seem unlikely to occur. Take, for instance, the decision of whether or not to sign up to donate one's organs upon death. Between the mid-1990s and early 2000s, almost 50,000 people died because they did not receive a suitable organ donation. The vast majority of Americans—almost 85 percent—approve of organ donation, but fewer than 30 percent take the steps to actually fill out an organ donation card (Johnson & Goldstein, 2003). I certainly fell into this category. I vividly remember the feeling of solemn responsibility when I first got my driver's license at the age of sixteen and was asked by the clerk at the Department of Motor Vehicles whether I wanted to register to donate my organs. This felt like something important I could do to help others, and I readily agreed. She handed me a card that I had to sign in the presence of two witnesses, have them sign, and then mail back to the DMV. All I had to do was have my mom and sister watch me sign the card and then put it in the mail—but somehow I kept forgetting, and the signature card languished in my wallet for years. I strongly believed in the moral imperative to be an organ donor, but I also strongly believed that I wasn't going to die for a long time, so it was never quite at the front of my mind to get the signatures and send the card in. It wasn't until I moved to another state—

Massachusetts—where the opt-in procedure just required my signature at the DMV that I became an organ donor.

Massachusetts switched me from an intended donor to one who was actually listed on the donor registry by reducing the hassles I had to deal with in order to follow through on my intentions. Several European countries have taken the more assertive step of establishing a national organ donation policy in which people are presumed to have consented to donate their organs unless they actively decide to opt out of donation. In countries with presumed donation policies, such as Austria, Belgium, and France, 98–99 percent of people remain on the donation registry. In countries where, like in the United States, people have to give explicit consent to donate their organs, fewer than 30 percent are on the registry. A particularly striking example of the effect of opt-in donation policies is Germany, where, despite sharing similar histories and cultural identities as Austria, only 12 percent of the population agrees to donate their organs (Johnson & Goldstein, 2003).

Changing the status quo in retirement planning and switching the default in organ donation decision making are both examples of concrete policy shifts: we change the rules for whether people have to opt in to or opt out of a program or policy, and that affects whether they participate. The *Office* anecdote I describe above is more of a shift in cultural norms: through messaging and publicity, we change people's sense of the possibilities that lie before them and the actions they need to take to realize these opportunities. A third type of leveraging the status quo is what I will refer to as meeting people where they are, that is, designing policies to engage students and families through actions they have already committed to, and using these opportunities to promote educational advancement (more on this in a moment). All three approaches have been used to steer students and families toward better educational outcomes. I begin by discussing ways in which concrete changes to the default condition have or could be harnessed in education and then turn to examining the power of cultural norms and meeting people where they are to affect students' educational outcomes.

## CHANGES TO THE STATUS QUO THROUGH
## DIRECT POLICY INTERVENTION

In recent years, educators and policy makers have experimented with changes to the default at various stages in students' lives—in high school and college, but also as early as kindergarten. San Francisco designed a particularly ambitious citywide initiative, Kindergarten to College, to help families get started on college savings as soon as their children enter the school system. Starting in the 2010–2011 academic year, the city opened college savings accounts for 1,200 kindergarten families and seeded each account with a $50 contribution. Students who qualified for free and reduced-price lunch received an additional $50 in their account. In subsequent years the city provided families with additional incentives to contribute to the account and incorporated financial literacy education into the school curriculum. Since the piloting of the program in the spring of 2011, San Francisco has expanded it to all 4,500 children who enroll in kindergarten each year, with 13,000 total accounts opened as of July 2014 (San Francisco Office of Financial Empowerment, 2014).

San Francisco's decision to establish a status quo where every kindergartener has a college savings account was motivated by several trends. First and foremost, the cost of college continues to climb rapidly. Even net of financial aid, many students and families face substantial financial gaps between their financial aid packages and the cost of attendance at their college, which they have to fill with personal savings and/or supplementary loans. Yet one in three children in San Francisco—and one in two Black and Latino children—is born into a family without any assets or savings (Phillips & Stuhldreher, 2011). Forty percent of San Francisco families have subprime credit scores, which can limit their access to financial savings products. A related concern is that a substantial share of students in San Francisco leave school before they can even consider a college education. Thirty-six percent of Black students and 22 percent of Latino students drop out before earning a high school diploma (Phillips & Stuhldreher, 2011).

Importantly, however, families' lack of accumulated savings is not for lack of intention or desire to save for their children's future. In a survey conducted with San Francisco families, nearly 100 percent of parents want to save for their child's college education, but only about half are able to follow through on this intention (Phillips & Stuhldreher, 2011). By setting up the college savings accounts, therefore, San Francisco created a default where all families were able to realize their desire to save for college. Beyond the initial $50 (or $100 for impoverished children) contribution, the city created additional incentives to encourage families to save for college. In a move hopefully more successful than Scott's Tots, private philanthropies agreed to a make a dollar-for-dollar match up to $100 for each contribution parents made to their account. Parents who signed up for an automatic contribution to the account or who made contributions for six straight months received an additional $100. Through the combination of establishing the accounts, seeding them with an initial contribution, and providing incentives for families to contribute, San Francisco's citywide policy promotes a status quo where college savings is the rule rather than the exception. Later in the chapter, I discuss how the Kindergarten to College program created powerful cultural norms for children and their families.

A lack of resources necessary to pay for higher education is not the only barrier that contributes to persistent socioeconomic inequalities in college access. Recent research suggests that as many as half of socioeconomically disadvantaged students do not apply to or attend the quality of institution (measured, for instance, by graduation rate) at which they have the academic credentials to be admitted. Among high-achieving students, only 34 percent of low-income students attend a selective college or university, compared with 78 percent of upper-income students.

One reason for these disparities may be that students are unaware how much colleges vary in both quality and affordability, net of financial aid, or that their high school performance qualifies them for admission at selective colleges and universities. Behavioral research also demonstrates that even small up-front cost obstacles can deter students from investing in important stages in the college application process, even if they recognize the long-term financial benefits of pursuing a college degree. For instance, when ACT Inc. changed its policy to allow ACT college entrance exam test takers to send their exams to four colleges for free instead of three, rather than incurring a $6 cost for the fourth choice, students applied to more colleges and low-income students were more likely to enroll at selective colleges (Pallais, forthcoming).

A more concrete barrier that contributes to persistent inequalities in college access and success is the college entrance exams themselves. Though some colleges are now SAT/ACT optional, college entrance exams remain a requirement for admission to the considerable majority of the nation's selective colleges and universities. Taking the SAT or ACT therefore makes students eligible to apply to these institutions, but there are added benefits as well. Both the SAT and ACT have search services where colleges can purchase students' names and send them promotional materials about their institution. Especially as more selective institutions strive for greater socioeconomic diversity on campus, low-income students with high test scores are likely to receive a considerable amount of recruitment materials, which may broaden their sense of the postsecondary possibilities that are available to them.

In order to take the SAT or ACT in most states, however, students must pay a fee (unless they qualify for and receive a fee waiver), and depending on where the exam is being offered, they may have to travel a considerable distance from their home to take the exam. Not surprisingly, given informational barriers about the benefits of taking a college entrance exam and the out-of-pocket and transportation costs associated with sitting for the test, only about two-thirds of high school students take the exam in a given year, with lower test-taking rates in economically disadvantaged communities (Hurwitz, Smith, Niu, & Howell, 2013).

Over the past decade, several states have changed the status quo so that taking a college entrance exam is mandatory for all students, rather than something students have to opt into. Colorado and Illinois were the earliest adopters; beginning in 2001, they required that all high school juniors take the ACT exam in the spring. Prior to this policy change, approximately 65 percent of students in each state took the exam (Goodman, 2012). The universal test-taking policy increased the share of students completing a college entrance exam to nearly 100 percent. Since then, several other states have made the ACT exam mandatory, while both Maine and Delaware now require all high school students to complete the SAT exam.

Establishing a default that all students must take a college entrance exam has led to meaningful improvements in college attendance rates. For instance, making the ACT mandatory in Colorado and Illinois increased enrollment at selective colleges and universities by approximately 20 percent (Goodman, 2012). Maine's mandatory SAT requirement increased attendance at four-year colleges and universities by approximately 5 percent, with effects largely driven by students who resided in small towns and rural areas of the state (Hurwitz et al., 2013). Interestingly, this pattern coincided with earlier research showing that the mismatch between students' academic achievement and the quality of institution that they apply to and attend is often most pronounced among high-achieving, low-income students residing in rural parts of the country (Hoxby & Avery, 2012).

Both of the policies to change defaults which I have described thus far had the goal of reducing the barriers to college attendance—either by increasing savings or by making certain that students took the entrance exams. Another set of policy defaults focuses on increasing the share of students who graduate from college, while reducing the time and number of courses it takes students to earn their diplomas. At a considerable majority of colleges and universities in the country, the status quo is that students have a high degree of choice in which courses and majors they pursue but unfortunately little access to in-depth advising to inform their course and major choices. In some community colleges, for instance, the ratio of advisors to students is as high as 1,500 to 1. In her seminal chapter "The Shapeless River," about the structural challenges that impede student success in community colleges, Judith Scott-Clayton ably sums up the challenge that college students face when confronted with too much course choice and too little advising: "They must choose how many courses to take and when to take them, based on course descriptions that may provide only partial information about course content and difficulty. . . . On top of this, students may have to make tradeoffs depending upon the vagaries of class schedules and work schedules. Logistically, just obtaining all of the information needed to make wise course choices can be difficult" (Scott-Clayton, 2015).

As we might expect, when faced with this choice complexity and lack of professional assistance, students struggle to make informed decisions about an effective course schedule. As a result, a substantial number of students who begin college full-time at two-year and four-year institutions do not earn a degree within three and six years, respectively. Among those who do earn a degree, the time it takes them to earn their diploma has increased over time. Furthermore, a substantial share of students take more total credits than they actually need to graduate, in part because students sometimes enroll in courses that do not count toward the degree they are pursuing. Of particular concern, there are wide socioeconomic disparities in college persistence and degree completion, even when comparing students with similar academic achievement (Bailey and Dynarski, 2012; Long & Mabel, 2012).

In response to these concerns, Complete College America (CCA), a non-profit organization focused on increasing college completion rates, has partnered with several colleges and universities to implement a set of defaults aimed at improving students' course selection—and thus their probability of earning a degree on time. Rather than put students in the position of making informed choices from the multitude of course options, CCA's partner institutions assign each freshman to an academic map based on the student's broad academic area of focus (science, technology, engineering, and math [STEM]; business; social sciences; etc.). Unlike most colleges, where students need to seek out an advisor's approval for the courses on their schedule, students are by default enrolled in the courses contained on their academic map. Students can choose to switch out of these courses, but doing so requires permission from an advisor. Each semester features a set of milestone courses that students have to take in the recommended sequence. For instance, a freshman in the STEM sequence might take English 101 and precalculus 101 milestone courses in the fall and English 102 and calculus 102 milestone courses in the spring. Students are required to meet with their advisors if they do not complete each milestone course in the intended semester. The default schedule for all students contains fifteen credits, which puts them on track to earn an associate's degree within two years or a bachelor's degree within four years.

Preliminary results suggest that the combination of academic maps and what CCA calls "intrusive advising" (when students fall off track) leads to positive effects on graduation rate and the time it takes students to earn a degree. At Georgia State University, for instance, which implemented the academic maps and intrusive advising, graduation rates increased by 20 percent over the decade in which these default policies were implemented, with particularly pronounced increases in graduation rates among underrepresented students. Florida State University similarly saw graduation rates increase after implementing degree maps and cut by half the number of students earning excess credits (Complete College America, 2014). It is worth noting that neither institution evaluated these policy changes experimentally, so it is possible that there were other concurrent initiatives happening at each university which contributed to these improved outcomes.

A recent experimental evaluation of the Accelerated Study in Associate Programs (ASAP), however, confirms that making highly structured course pathways the status quo experience for students can have substantial impacts on their academic success (Scrivener & Weiss, 2013). ASAP operates at community colleges in the City University of New York (CUNY) system. Adopting similar approaches to those at Georgia State and Florida State, ASAP requires students to carry a full-time course load. Students are scheduled as a group to take a preestablished set of courses during their first year. ASAP students similarly receive intensive advising. Early experimental results are quite promising: students randomly assigned to ASAP earned 25 percent more credits after two years than students in the control group; ASAP students were also 66 percent more likely to earn a degree within several years of starting the program.

Unfortunately, defaults do not always work in students' favor. Student loan repayment is one such example. Student indebtedness has emerged as a top concern for both policy makers and the general public. Students are borrowing more over time to finance their college education, while default rates have nearly doubled over the past decade (Project on Student Debt, 2013). Consequences of defaulting are severe for borrowers, who are subject to wage garnishments and withholding of other government disbursements.

Accelerating student borrowing and loan defaulting are particularly problematic among community college students, who have increasingly turned to loans to finance their education. The proportion of community college students taking out education loans rose from 12.1 percent in 1992–1993 to 25.5 percent in 2007–2008 (National Center for Education Statistics, 2012). The average full-time community college student borrower took out $4,800 in student loans in 2010–2011, which is nearly double the average cost of tuition at a community college (National Center for Education Statistics, 2013). Community college students have a high default rate on loans, with 20.9 percent defaulting within three years of entering repayment (Federal Student Aid, 2014b).

There have also been recent media reports that suggest that carrying substantial loan burden can inhibit students from making other important investments in their lives (like buying a home) or from pursuing certain career paths, which in turn may have negative impacts on the economy (El-Boghdady, 2014).

In response to these escalating default rates, the federal government has introduced several loan repayment options to provide eligible borrowers with more flexibility about how they manage their monthly payments (Federal Student Aid, 2014a). Under the Income-Based Repayment Plan, for instance, monthly payments are set at a maximum of 15 percent of individuals' discretionary income in a given time period. After twenty-five years, any remaining balance on the loan is forgiven. The terms of the Pay As You Earn Plan are similar, but that plan caps monthly payments at 10 percent of discretionary income with balance forgiveness at the end of twenty years. These plans are not without their downsides. Borrowers may end up paying more overall than under the ten-year standard plan, and they risk paying income tax on any amount forgiven at the end of the loan period. However, these plans do give borrowers the flexibility to manage payments on top of other expenses when their income is limited.

The challenge, however, is that the default plan in which federal loan borrowers are enrolled is the standard repayment plan. This loan repayment option works much like a fixed-rate mortgage, with students maintaining a set interest rate and making fixed payments throughout the life of the loan (typically ten to twenty years). While standard repayment loans allow students to pay off their loan in the shortest amount of time and require them to pay the least interest over the life of the loan, monthly payments are typically higher, particularly for borrowers who qualify for one of the income-based repayment options.

In order to help borrowers stay on top of their payments, the federal government has made a concerted effort to increase public awareness about income-based repayment plans. This has included direct e-mail campaigns to borrowers to inform them about income-based repayment options, as well as advertisements through tax preparation sites such as TurboTax and H&R Block. Loan servicers—the organizations that the U.S. Department of Education (USDOE) contracts to manage students' loan repayments—also reach out to borrowers to inform them of income-based repayment options. Still, students must initiate a request to switch from a standard repayment plan to one of the income-based repayment alternatives.

And yet, evaluating loan repayment options is a cognitively demanding task, and switching plans requires students to complete additional loan-related processes and paperwork. It is not surprising that, as of the third quarter of 2013, only 6 percent of borrowers were signed up for the Income-Based Repayment or Pay As You Earn repayment options (Delisle, 2014). There are indications that these programs are growing more popular among borrowers: by the third quarter of 2014, just over 10 percent of borrowers had selected one of these plans (Delisle, 2014). But it certainly stands to reason that if, instead of being automatically enrolled in the standard repayment plan, students had to make an active choice about which loan repayment option would best suit their circumstances (perhaps at the point of first signing up for the loan, and again upon leaving college), more students would opt for one of the income-based repayment alternatives.

### CHANGING THE STATUS QUO BY SHIFTING CULTURAL NORMS

Another approach to changing the status quo focuses less on concrete and immediate changes to the programs in which people participate and instead strives to change people's perceptions of their own status quo. In the *Office* episode, Michael's impulsive (and, ultimately, unfulfilled) promise to pay college tuition for an entire third grade class didn't result in any immediate change to their educational experience or the resources they could access to succeed in school. Michael's promise did, however, profoundly shift the students' view about their own future possibilities.

Here was a Scranton businessman who believed in them so much that he was willing to give his own money to help them go to college. Michael's confidence in the students may have resulted in two important shifts in students' outlook. First, among many economically disadvantaged students and families, the default view is that a college education is something that they cannot afford. Students and parents from lower-income backgrounds tend to substantially overestimate the cost of college net of financial aid they would likely qualify for (Avery & Kane, 2004; Grodsky & Jones, 2007; Horn, Chen, & Chapman, 2003). Michael Scott introduced a new norm, where college would be free so long as they worked hard and graduated from high school.

Second, students who are the first in their family to go to college or who are from racial or ethnic backgrounds traditionally underrepresented in college may not feel that they belong at colleges if they perceive these institutions to be the domain of affluent, White students (Walton & Cohen,

2007). They may also be concerned that they would need to downplay their group identity in order to succeed in college (Cohen & Garcia, 2005). As students progress in school, uncertainty about whether they would fit in on campus may result in greater stress, impeding their ability to focus on completing important college- and financial-aid-related tasks (Lovelace & Rosen, 1996). Michael's confidence in these students may have helped to combat these doubts by priming positive identities about their own capacity for collegiate success (Ross, White, Wright, & Knapp, 2013). The Scott's Tots promise may have helped shift students' status quo from "I'm not someone who could succeed in college" to "I'm someone who is going to college." We'll return to this powerful idea of identity priming in chapter 4.

Fortunately, efforts to change cultural norms exist outside of the realm of TV sitcoms, and many share Michael Scott's vision of changing students' and families' beliefs about whether college has a place in their future. Earlier I described the San Francisco Kindergarten to College program as a concrete change in policy, since the city automatically enrolled all kindergarteners in a college savings plan. But in reality, even with the matching incentives in place, most families may struggle over time to accumulate sufficient savings to cover the unmet financial gap they may face between financial aid and the cost of attendance at whatever college they decide to attend. The more impactful feature of the citywide college savings plan may, instead, have been instilling a belief among families that college was a viable option for their children (Ross et al., 2013). For instance, by setting up the college savings account on behalf of all kindergarteners, the city may have primed both the child and their parents to believe that going to college was an expected future outcome. Students may work harder in school in order to fulfill this expectation. Parents may make additional contributions to the account to help secure a college education for their child. Increased efforts by the child and parent likely reinforce each other: the student works harder to make good on their parents' contributions, while the parents contribute more when they see how hard their child is working in school (Ross et al., 2013). In addition, the college savings accounts provide a channel through which the city can help make a postsecondary education vivid and relatable for children and their families. Every time families receive a letter or log in to make a contribution is an opportunity to provide concrete and visual descriptions of their future lives. Especially for families who do not have personal college experience, these cues can help students visualize and internalize the future possibilities in which they are investing (Ross et al., 2013).

The Knowledge Is Power Program (KIPP) national network of public charter schools incorporates the idea of changing cultural norms into much of their daily practice with students (KIPP, 2014).[1] Starting in kindergarten, students' classrooms are named based on the college their teacher attended. "Towson State!" the teacher will call, "time to line up for lunch." College pennants adorn classroom walls. Students learn the cheers and fight songs from their teacher's alma mater. Succeeding in college is woven in as a goal throughout daily conversations with students and families. Teachers ask students to tuck their uniform shirts in because "you're going to be expected to look professional when you're in college." During conferences with parents, teachers constantly reinforce that the high academic expectations and extended school day and year are all focused on preparing students to succeed in college. As students progress toward middle and high school, they are referred to not by their graduating high school class but rather by the year when their class is expected to graduate from college. Implicit in this approach is the recognition that students are likely to work harder—and therefore academic instruction will be more effective—when they believe that college is a very real and accessible option they can pursue.

And of course, Scott's Tots has its basis in actual "promise" scholarship programs that are now offered in communities across the country. One of the first places to offer a promise scholarship was Kalamazoo, Michigan. At a surprise announcement on November 10, 2005, then-superintendent Janice Brown revealed that an anonymous group of donors had committed to paying 100 percent of college tuition at public institutions in the state for any child who had attended Kalamazoo Public Schools since kindergarten.[2] Unlike most financial aid programs, which are awarded based on academic merit or financial need, the Kalamazoo Promise scholarship was given to any student who met the residency requirements and who was accepted to college.

On one level it may be more appropriate to think of Kalamazoo Promise—and programs like it across the country—as a concrete change in policy. Instead of students and families having to pay tuition, the new status quo was that a group of anonymous donors would pay for the cost of college. The Promise scholarships clearly have this component. But the actual pay-off of this shift in policy isn't received until the end of the student's senior year. What may be equally important is the abrupt change in the cultural norm catalyzed by the Promise scholarship.

Once home to factories making everything from Gibson guitars to Checker cabs and Upjohn pharmaceuticals, by the early 2000s Rust Belt Kalamazoo was in a steady economic decline (Fishman, 2012). One-third of students in the Kalamazoo Public Schools lived below the federal poverty line, nearly one in ten was homeless, and the city had the highest rate of teen pregnancy among African American young women in the state. Many families struggled to make ends meet from week to week, let alone put away money for college. School enrollments had steadily declined since the mid-1980s, especially among White students (Bartik & Lachowska, 2014). In Kalamazoo, as in many impoverished cities, the default path for a large share of youth was to drop out of school before high school graduation.

For a moment, put yourself in the shoes of a high school junior in Kalamazoo who had done well in school and was motivated to continue her education. Getting into college would have required that student to take a series of actions that ran counter to the status quo: staying in school when classmates were dropping out, working on applications and college essays when friends were searching for jobs, contemplating leaving home for college when almost everyone else in your social circle was staying in Kalamazoo. Some students have the drive and perseverance to persist on the path to college even in the face of these strong competing pressures—but as we've seen, many others may instead opt for the path of least resistance, even if they have strong potential to succeed in higher education.

The Kalamazoo Promise provided a much-needed shock to this cultural status quo. As Ted Fishman reported in the *New York Times Magazine*, the community reacted with intense joy and gratitude after hearing Superintendent Brown's surprise announcement. As one father told Mr. Fishman, "After the Promise was announced on the 11 o'clock news, the kids were up celebrating until two or three in the morning. We kept waiting for someone to say it was a joke." Another high school student recalled, "It was my sixth-grade year when the donations were made and officially announced. I'm pretty sure that my mother cried" (Fishman, 2012).

The Kalamazoo Public Schools experienced an immediate uptick in enrollment and a lasting decline over the years in the number of students who exited the school system. Following the Promise, the share of students earning any high school credits increased markedly, while the number of days students spent in suspension declined substantially. Effects were particularly pronounced for African American students, who also experienced a considerable increase in their academic performance (as measured by GPAs; Bartik & Lachowska, 2014). The Kalamazoo Promise has not been a panacea—African American males continue to graduate at lower rates than their peers, and while the vast majority of high school graduates pursue higher education, college persistence continues to be a challenge. Yet these are hurdles that many communities continue to face. By disrupting the status quo, the Kalamazoo Promise established a new cultural norm for the city: stay in school, stay out of trouble, and go to college.

## MEETING PEOPLE WHERE THEY ARE

So far in the chapter we've seen how concrete changes to whether people have to opt into or out of a program can affect their participation in a program and, as a result, their outcomes. We've also seen how shifting people's perceptions of cultural norms or what they can expect can affect their engagement in education. A different approach to leveraging the status quo is to meet people where they are at, that is, to recognize activities in which people are already engaging as part of their daily routines as opportunities to improve their educational outcomes. The goal of meeting people where they are is to help them overcome obstacles that can prevent access to beneficial programs.

In the behavioral economics literature, these obstacles are sometimes referred to as hassle factors. Marianne Bertrand, Sendhil Mullainathan, and Eldar Shafir (2004) offer the example of food stamp applications as a hassle factor that can deter families from receiving important nutritional assistance. At the time of the authors' report, state food stamp applications were up to thirty-six pages long. Applicants had to submit to fingerprinting to ensure they weren't trying to sign up for food stamps in multiple locations, and in some settings they had to undergo home visits to confirm their impoverishment. In a standard cost-benefit analysis, the costs, broadly speaking, of completing the application process should be far lower than the benefits that accrue as a result of doing so. In the realm of actual decision making, however, hassle factors can often deter people from doing things that would result in clear benefits for them.

People are more likely to follow through on otherwise challenging tasks if doing so is built into something they are already engaging in as a matter of practice. Take, for instance, the challenge of improving early literacy among children from economically disadvantaged families. Low-income children tend to be exposed to considerably less reading before they enter formal child care settings. This, in turn, has given rise to what is now commonly known as the "word gap." One pioneering study conducted in the early 1990s found that low-income children had heard thirty million fewer words by the age of three than their more affluent peers (Risley & Hart, 1995). More recent research by psychologist Anne Fernald shows that, as early as eighteen months, children from more affluent families can identify pictures of simple words at a substantially more rapid rate than lower-income children (Fernald, Marchman, & Weisleder, 2013). Proponents for universal pre-K have highlighted both studies as evidence for the importance of expanding access to quality child care for all children. While universal pre-K programs have emerged in some municipalities and states, they can be expensive to implement, and legislation to expand universal pre-K access has yet to gain traction at the federal level. How, then, can policy makers promote more active reading to young children in low-income communities?

Another way of asking this question is, "Where can we meet low-income parents to provide them with books and information about the importance of early reading?" One answer is the pediatrician's office. Parents and their infants typically visit their pediatrician multiple times a year during the first three years of life for wellness visits. Reach Out and Read, a nonprofit organization, recognized that these visits provided an opportunity not only to ensure that children were physically healthy but also to give free books and promote the importance of parents reading regularly to their children. The program, which began in 1989 in one hospital in Boston, now operates in all fifty states and distributes books and early literacy guidance to four million children each year (Reach Out and Read, 2014). Various research studies indicate that children who are exposed to Reach Out and Read are read to more frequently by their parents, have more books in their home, and perform higher on language and vocabulary tests.[3] Under a new policy enacted in June 2014, the American Academy of Pediatrics now recommends that all its members advocate for parents reading aloud to their infants (Rich, 2014).

Another way to meet low-income parents where they are at in order to promote early literacy is through the television. PBS has been doing this for nearly a half century with programs such as *Sesame Street*. More recently, Too Small to Fail, a joint venture between the Bill, Hillary & Chelsea Clinton Foundation and Next Generation focused on promoting health and well-being for children under age five, announced a partnership with Univision, an American Spanish-language television broadcast channel, to develop early literacy content for viewers. Univision is now the most highly viewed network in the country, even surpassing NBC, CBS, ABC, and Fox, providing reach to tens of millions of viewers each month—including millions of viewers with young children (Moreno, 2014). The initiative, titled *Pequeños y Valiosos* (Young and Valuable), will integrate advice for Hispanic parents and caregivers to read aloud to children into Univision programming, including segments on the network's top morning show and its nightly evening news program.

Reducing hassles may also be important to address the rising trend of childhood obesity in the United States. A third of the U.S. population is now obese, and in 2013, forty-three million preschoolers were overweight or obese—a 60 percent rise since 1990 (Harvard School of Public Health, 2014). Strategies to address the obesity epidemic range from motivational (First Lady Michelle Obama's Let's Move campaign to promote more exercise) to regulatory (former New York City mayor Michael Bloomberg's campaign to ban the sale of jumbo-sized sugary drinks). But if there's one place to influence the eating habits of American children, it's the school cafeteria. Tens of millions of children pass through their school's cafeteria every day, which provides a powerful opportunity to promote healthier eating habits.

Earlier in the chapter, we saw how Chili's installed smart tablets in its restaurants. Throughout the meal, diners are subtly prompted to make additional orders: when they sit down, diners are presented with images of heaping plates of nachos; halfway through the meal, they see images of mouth-watering desserts. It turns out that we're much more likely to purchase appetizers and desserts when, rather than waiting for a server to appear, we can satisfy our impulses with the push of a button. According to Ziosk, the company that operates the tablets in Chili's restaurants, sales of appetizers and desserts increased by 20 percent after the tablets were installed (Garber, 2014). The same types of impulses exist in many cafeterias. As students wait in line to pay at the register, they are typically presented with a range of snack foods and dessert options they can add to their meal. Sales of these products can generate important revenue for school lunch programs but also obviously add unhealthy items to students' trays. In a Minnesota school, researchers David Just and Brian Wansink co-opted students' tendency to make impulse purchases at the register line by replacing the snack and dessert items with fruit. Students still made impulse purchases while they waited to pay, but now they were adding something healthy. The researchers report that fruit sales increased, snack sales decreased, and overall revenue to the school lunch program was unaffected (Just & Wansink, 2009).

Another creative strategy that school cafeterias have employed to improve students' nutrition is to simply shift the position of the salad bar. In many cafeterias the salad bar is off to the side, so students don't encounter it unless they actively seek it out (not surprisingly, most students do not). A middle school in Corning, New York, instead put the salad bar in the middle of the cafeteria so that students had to encounter it in order to get to other food options. Even if for a split second, students now had to actively consider the salad bar, if for no other reason than to think about how to get around it to what they really wanted. Just and Wansink report that this minor shift—literally putting healthy food directly in their path—led to an immediate and persistent increase in the number of salad items purchased.

Earlier we saw how a change in policy requiring all high school juniors to take the SAT or ACT college entrance exam can lead to meaningful improvements in college enrollment. One barrier that these policies overcome is students having to travel outside of their home community in order to take the exams. As an alternative to making college entrance exams mandatory for all students, another option states can pursue is to bring the exam to students rather than require students to travel to them. Economist George Bulman studied the impact of high schools opening new test centers on whether students completed the SAT or ACT and enrolled in college. He found that the ability to take the test in one's own school increased test taking by over 8 percent, and that these students completed as much college as the average test taker at their school (Bulman, 2012).

Meeting students and families where they are can also help more low-income students and their families qualify for financial aid for college. The Free Application for Federal Student Aid (FAFSA), which students must complete to qualify for most financial aid, is widely recognized as a roadblock on the road to college for economically disadvantaged students. The application requires students and families to answer a complicated set of questions about their income, assets, and family composition. It is a model of bureaucratic complexity and reminds one of filing your taxes (in the days before TurboTax!). The FAFSA itself may deter hundreds of thousands of academically ready students from entering college in the first place or from persisting after they have enrolled (Bird & Castleman, 2014; Dynarski & Scott-Clayton, 2006; King, 2004; Kofoed, 2013).

This recognition has led to a multitude of initiatives to provide students with additional information about and assistance with the financial aid process. These include the USDOE FAFSA Completion Pilot, which provides school districts with data about whether students have completed the FAFSA, and privately funded events such as College Goal Sunday, where students and their families can get assistance with completing the FAFSA. While I am a strong proponent of both of these efforts, it is worth noting that their success depends on active participation by schools, counselors, students, and their families. The USDOE FAFSA Completion Pilot depends on schools using the data to communicate with students about their FAFSA and on students remembering to bring in all the necessary tax documents to work on their applications. Events like College Goal Sunday rely on students and families (1) knowing they exist and (2) taking time out of a weekend to go to the event location and meet with a financial aid counselor. It still has a high hassle factor.

A different approach is to help families with FAFSA completion in a setting where they have already chosen to come with all the necessary paperwork—namely, tax preparation offices. Economists Eric Bettinger, Bridget Terry Long, Phil Oreopoulos, and Lisa Sanbonmatsu (2012) collaborated with H&R Block to integrate FAFSA completion into the tax return process. The researchers worked with H&R Block to design software that would allow tax preparers to prepopulate the FAFSA with information that families had already provided while completing their tax returns. Remarkably, completing the FAFSA required less than ten minutes of additional time, yet it led to a substantial increase not only in the amount of financial aid students received but also in whether students enrolled and persisted in college (Bettinger et al., 2012).

## REMOVING THE ROADBLOCKS

We've seen how, in the face of complex information and complicated choices, students and families struggle to make informed decisions about their educational choices. In this chapter, we saw one common response to complexity: simply failing to make any choice at all. In many situations, the failure to make a choice means that people wind up with the default outcome—not taking college entrance exams, continuing to eat unhealthy foods in the school cafeteria, and so on. Changing the default—through any of the approaches I've discussed in this chapter—accounts for this tendency to stick with the status quo and can promote better decision making. Next, we turn to a different set of strategies for promoting better decisions. Through a combination of prompts, planning assistance, and strategies designed to get people to commit to their intentions, we can encourage people to make active choices rather than put them off and find themselves stuck in the status quo.

# Chapter 3
. . . . . . . . . . . . . . . .
## Encouraging
## Active Decisions

IN EARLY 2014, things were not looking good for the Affordable Care Act (ACA). The Obama administration had forecast that six million people would sign up for an insurance plan by the March 31 deadline, but—owing in part to technical difficulties with the Healthcare.gov website—just over four million had enrolled by the end of February (U.S. Department of Health and Human Services, 2014b). Of particular concern were the comparatively low enrollment rates among younger Americans. As of February, fewer than 30 percent of people who had signed up for health insurance under ACA were under the age of 35 (U.S. Department of Health and Human Services, 2014b). According to popular wisdom, the success of the plan hinged on ensuring strong enrollment among this age group.[1] Because younger people tend to be healthier, the premiums they pay often exceed the costs of health care they incur. This surplus could be used to offset the greater health expenses incurred by older Americans and in turn curb growth in insurance premiums from one year to the next. As James Surowiecki described in a March 31 *New Yorker* column, critics foretold that the lower enrollment rates among younger Americans would result in a "death spiral" for ACA (Surowiecki, 2014): health costs would exceed premiums paid by enrollees (mainly older Americans), which would require insurance companies to raise premiums. These higher premiums would further deter younger Americans from signing up for plans. Costs would continue to rise, and the system would soon be financially bankrupt.

Sluggish enrollment among American youth was not for lack of effort by the Obama administration and supporters of ACA. As Surowiecki reported, in the months leading up to the March enrollment deadline, administration staff and congressional allies blanketed college campuses across the country, touting the economic and health benefits of signing up for insurance under ACA. Both the administration and state-run insurance exchanges ran extensive ad campaigns targeting Americans ages 18–34 to promote the importance of enrolling in an ACA insurance plan. One explanation for the lack of responsiveness among younger citizenry is that people were just putting off the onerous task of enrolling for health insurance in favor of more immediate or enjoyable pursuits (much like putting off exercising in favor of getting more sleep in the morning). This inclination to procrastinate was undoubtedly magnified by the extensive media coverage of the glitches plaguing the website and the time people spent trying to sign up for a plan, only to have the site crash on them.

Another explanation, however, is that the Obama administration wasn't using the right communications channels to reach young people. Speeches on college campuses reach some young people, but many students who are interested enough to attend a speech about health care probably would have signed up for a plan anyway. Ad campaigns for ACA, even if delivered through social media platforms, had to compete with the tidal wave of other ads and content that confront us every time we log on to Instagram, Facebook, and Twitter.

Recognizing the need to change their approach, the administration took a novel (and behaviorally informed) approach: have Obama himself bring ACA to the students. On the evening of March 11, 2014, President Obama made an appearance on *Between Two Ferns*, an online mock interview show hosted by Zack Galifianakis on FunnyorDie.com. As Dan Pfieffer, a senior advisor to President Obama, told the *Huffington Post* following the interview, "We have to find ways to break through. This is essentially an extension of the code we have been trying to crack for seven years now" (Alman, 2014). The president had to endure a string of absurd and comical questions (for example, whether he would be building his presidential library "in your home country of Kenya"), which he took good-naturedly. But appearing on the show also gave him the opportunity to speak to a large audience of young people and to make the case for why they should sign up for health insurance under ACA: "Healthcare.gov works great now and millions of Americans have already gotten health insurance plans," the President said. "And what we want is for people to know that you can get affordable health care and most young Americans, right now they're not covered and the truth is they can get coverage all for what it costs to pay your cell phone bill" (*Chicago Tribune*, 2014). The video went viral—and more importantly, the strategy worked. Many of the people watching the show were prompted to learn more about their insurance options. As Tara McGuinness, a senior communications advisor, tweeted that evening, "FunnyorDie.com is the #1 source of referrals to http://HealthCare.gov right now."

Whether it was the president's appearance on *Between Two Ferns*, or a host of other efforts to reach this demographic (for example, enlisting famous basketball players and even the mothers of celebrities to tout the plan), or simply the fact that young adults were waiting until the last minute to sign up for insurance, enrollments among this age group increased 15 percent in the month before the deadline. This surge helped to fuel over seven million total enrollments by the end of March (U.S. Department of Health and Human Services, 2014c).

The apparent impact of President Obama's *Between Two Ferns* appearance on ACA enrollment illustrates several principles about how people make decisions—whether about health insurance, financial savings, lifestyle choices, or education. One of the core behavioral principles that the ACA example highlights is the strong tendency many of us have to privilege present demands over future intentions. It's quite possible that many of the people—both young and old—who eventually enrolled in an insurance plan in March had planned to do so for months. Some may have even told themselves, "I know I need to do this. Next week I'll set aside the three hours it's going to take to get it done—even if I have to miss *Monday Night Football*." But when next week arrives, the appeal of *Monday Night Football* invariably wins out over enrolling in a health plan—even if the person recognizes that having health coverage is in her best interests. Economists refer to this seeming contradiction in our priorities as *time-inconsistent preferences*. Looking forward to the next week, the same person thinks she will set aside time for health insurance because she values it more than *Monday Night Football* in the future, but when Monday evening arrives, her love of the New England Patriots wins out once again.

Second, simply making information available about programs is rarely sufficient. This is the "if we build it, they will come" fallacy we looked at earlier, which still characterizes the approach of a surprising number of policy initiatives. Especially in the age of the Internet, the information that people need to make informed decisions—whether about health insurance, purchasing a car, or choosing a school for their child—is only a click away on their computer. But just because information is *available* does not mean that people will access it. People may not know that information is readily available—or at a more basic level, that an important decision (like whether to sign up for health insurance or face a financial penalty) is looming before them.

Even when policy makers communicate information about an important program, they may not choose effective channels for communicating, or they fail to convey aspects of the decision that are most salient to people. Fifty years before President Obama appeared on *Between Two Ferns*, psychologists Howard Leventhal, Robert Singer, and Susan Jones (1965) illustrated the importance of getting both the message and medium right in the context of increasing the number of Yale University students who got tetanus vaccinations. Neither straightforward information (a booklet about tetanus transmission) nor scare tactics like showing graphic images of people suffering with tetanus motivated students to get vaccinated. These were smart students, after all—they probably already saw the value in getting tetanus shots. On the other hand, subjects who received a campus map showing the location of the health center were considerably more likely to get vaccinated. As it turned out, boosting vaccination rates simply required providing students with a visual cue of where they could go to get their tetanus shot.

Even when we know that a decision has to be made and want to seek out information to make an informed choice, we aren't always very good about freeing up time and attention from everything else to focus on the decision. Many readers have probably had the experience of remembering they need to do something important only at inopportune times—such as just before you fall asleep—when it's not actually possible to deal with the task. Incidentally, the fact that we remember at these moments may be precisely *because* we have slowed down and our prospective memories have more capacity to recall the tasks we didn't quite get to during our busy days (Dismukes, 2012; Ross, White, Wright, & Knapp, 2013).

An additional challenge people face is making judgments about how long they'll need to complete a task. Many people substantially underestimate the actual time it takes to complete complicated processes like signing up for health insurance (or writing a book, for that matter) (Buehler, Griffin, & Ross, 1994). We also overestimate the number of tasks we believe we can complete in a given time period. This unrealistic optimism can reinforce our tendency to put off tasks since we assume we'll still have time to finish them before the deadline.

President Obama's appearance on *Between Two Ferns* responded to each of these behavioral principles. He communicated information about ACA health insurance plans through a channel trusted by the group he wanted to reach. He made health insurance salient by weaving it into witty back-and-forth banter with Zack Galifianakis. He prompted people to visit Healthcare .gov while they were already online watching the show. The latter point is particularly worth emphasizing. As we saw earlier, even minor hassles like having to go online to complete a task can deter people from following through on their intentions. It's quite possible that some of the people who were inspired to visit Healthcare.gov while watching *Between Two Ferns* would not have done so if they were viewing the program on their televisions rather than on their computers.

Political strategists aren't the only ones applying behavioral insights to influence decisions people make. Long before behavioral economics was in vogue in public policy circles, the private sector capitalized on these principles to sell their products and services. Advertisers have known for decades that it's not enough to just develop colorful catalogs or websites with their products and assume that customers will appear. The private sector takes a much more intrusive approach to influencing which goods and services we buy, investing millions in advertising to make their products attractive and to create a sense of purchasing urgency.

I was recently struck by the sheer power of this advertising on a JetBlue flight with my children. We watch videos at home, but mainly on Netflix or Amazon Prime, so my kids rarely see commercials. On the three-hour flight to Florida they were glued to the Nickelodeon channel on DirecTV. They enjoyed the television programs but were absolutely mesmerized by the commercials. Their attention was riveted by the combination of fast-moving images and upbeat music. The scenes of other kids their age having the time of their lives playing with the toys featured in the commercial were nothing short of intoxicating to them. After every commercial, they said, "Daddy, I really need that," and I think they meant it in a very literal way. A thirty-second commercial was so powerfully designed that my children felt that their happiness depended on having that product. The good news, of course, is that my kids are young enough that out of sight is out of mind. By the time we got off the plane, they had forgotten about the commercials— or at least I think they are out of their mind. Advertisers also work to build brand recognition, and I'm sure some of that remains with my kids as it does with all of us.

And of course, the private sector is always at the frontier of leveraging trending communications channels. Long before most schools or nonprofit organizations had their own websites, Coke, Nike, and every other major company were already well on their way toward developing a sophisticated online presence. The same goes for Facebook and Pinterest pages and Twitter and Instagram feeds. These same companies were also the first to see the power of text messaging as a means of engaging people in interactive communication—think how long it's been that fans have been able to vote for their favorite *American Idol* singer by texting a number to Fox Television.

Fortunately, the past several years have witnessed a concerted effort by policy makers and researchers to co-opt these approaches to nudge people toward better social outcomes. In the sections that follow we'll look at different strategies to help people make more informed decisions and to follow through on intentions they have set for themselves. These interventions draw on some combination of the following themes: prompting people to focus their attention on important actions or decisions, using effective channels to deliver information, providing people with concrete ways to translate their intentions into actions, and framing choices in ways that are more likely to elicit a response.

## THE POWER OF PROMPTS

Prompts to take action or follow through on our intentions are powerful because they directly address some of the barriers that prevent people from making informed decisions: our tendency to procrastinate when faced with complex decisions, our bias toward the present, and our difficulty maintaining attention when balancing other competing demands in our lives. Prompts can operate through various channels to encourage more active decisions: they can help us combat procrastination by creating a sense of urgency around a task we have been putting off. For instance, reminding a high school senior in mid-February that they only have two weeks to complete the financial aid application by March 1 in order to qualify for additional aid may help spur students and their families to invest the time necessary to complete the application. Prompts can make clear connections between our future goals and present choices. Seeing calorie counts on menus in fast-food restaurants, for example, prompts us to remember our weight loss goals and may lead us to pick healthier choices (Bleich, Barry, Gary-Webb, & Herring, 2014). And prompts can help us focus on completing a task in the moment, before our attention moves elsewhere.

Of course, for prompts to be effective, they have to be delivered through channels that effectively reach people. What has struck me over the course of my own research is how many organizations send out important information about valuable programs through media that just don't reach a substantial share of their target population. I've often wondered how many of the millions of e-mails chock full with informative content are sitting unopened in in-boxes across the country, their usefulness drowned by the sheer volume of daily messages that people receive. Only 3 percent of teenagers report exchanging e-mails on a daily basis (Lenhart, 2012). There's a reason that Nike doesn't rely anymore on postal mail catalogs or e-mail blasts to sell sneakers.

By contrast, even a few simple prompts that leverage effective communications channels can be surprisingly influential on decision making. In the health care sector, for instance, researchers have used a variety of creative techniques to help people progress toward healthier lifestyles. One challenge that physicians often encounter is patients' lack of adherence to medications that have been prescribed to them. For a wide range of medicines, not taking the dose on a consistent schedule (for example, 5:00 p.m. every afternoon) can reduce their efficacy. Now, for most people, failure to take their medication on a set schedule is not an indication that they don't want to get better or don't think that the medication is beneficial—it's just that it can be hard to remember to take pills at the same time each day. Think about a single parent who's been at work all day, rushes to pick up the kids from school, and then is scrambling to throw dinner together. Is it really any surprise if the parent doesn't remember each day to take their pill right at 5:00 p.m.? The challenge of adhering to a medication schedule is a perfect illustration of how inattention can negatively affect people's outcomes. One company's solution to this problem was to design a special kind of pill bottle that glows and beeps if it is not opened at the same time each day (Mullainathan, 2011). For many people these simple visual and audible cues are all that they need to remember a task. Results from a randomized trial indicate that, three months after medication was prescribed, 98–99 percent of patients who were given Glow Cap pill containers adhered to their medication, compared to only 52 percent of patients in the control group (Vitality, 2014).

Public health researchers have also made extensive use of text messaging to help people follow through on health-related goals they set. Text messaging may arguably be the most effective communications channel currently available to policy makers and researchers. Nearly two-thirds of the world's population has a mobile phone, and 75 percent of cell phone subscribers across twenty-one different countries report regularly sending and receiving texts (Head, Noar, Iannarino, & Grant Harrington, 2013). It will come as no surprise to anyone who has teenage children that texting is particularly popular among adolescents. As evidence of the changing currents of communication, 65 percent of teenagers report texting with each other on a daily basis (Lenhart, 2012). Another advantage of text messaging is its cost-effectiveness. The cost of message delivery can be as little as a penny or less per message (Castleman & Page, 2015), and while there can be up-front costs associated with the design of a text message delivery system, it's nonetheless possible to send text messages to thousands of recipients over a several-month duration for only a few dollars per recipient (Castleman & Page, 2015; Castleman & Page, forthcoming). Text message prompts have been used to support people in achieving a range of positive health outcomes, from quitting smoking and exercising more regularly to losing weight and keeping medical appointments (Head et al., 2013).

In one study involving over 9,000 low-income children ranging in age from six months to eighteen years, researchers sent text messages to a randomly selected group of parents reminding them to get flu vaccines (Stockwell et al., 2012). Several of the messages emphasized vaccine safety and the health risks associated with getting the flu. Others messages provided parents with information about the hours and location of clinics where they could get a vaccination. To make the messages as meaningful as possible to recipients (and therefore maximize the likelihood that they would act on the prompt), the content was personalized to each recipient—information about health risks was customized to the age of the child, and messages were even translated into the parents' preferred language. This small handful of text message prompts increased flu vaccination rates by nearly 10 percent.

Similar messaging prompts have been used in other policy arenas to help people achieve personally and socially beneficial goals. Economists Dean Karlan, Margaret McConnell, Sendhil Mullainathan, and Jonathan Zinman (2010) investigated whether monthly reminders could increase financial savings rates in the developing world. Working in partnership with banks in the Philippines, Bolivia, and Peru, the authors randomly assigned people who had signed up for a savings account at the bank to receive reminders via either text messages (Philippines and Bolivia) or letters (Peru, where there was low cell phone usage) to make deposits to their accounts. Several months after individuals had opened their accounts, customers across the three countries who received the reminders had saved 6 percent more than their counterparts who did not receive the messages. The Peruvian experiment featured a particularly interesting extension in which customers were assigned to one of two treatment groups: the first group received the standard reminders, while the second group received a reminder that explicitly referred to how much the person had indicated they planned to save when they opened their account. Customers who received the reminder of their initial savings goal saved 16 percent more than customers who did not receive any reminder.[2] This suggests that tying reminders to specific and concrete goals people have set for themselves may increase their ability to accomplish those goals.

## LEVERAGING TEXT MESSAGING TO
## IMPROVE EDUCATIONAL OUTCOMES

Text messaging prompts have become increasingly popular in education and have been used at all levels of schooling—even to build a foundation for literacy among babies barely old enough to sit up on their own. As we learned earlier, poverty imposes forms of scarcity on people: a lack of adequate housing or nutrition, a lack of safety, and a lack of cognitive bandwidth.[3] Reduced bandwidth means that people have less attention to devote overall to any one task—such as parents remembering to read to their children. Text message prompts can serve the helpful function of reminding parents to make time each day to read to their children. Another challenge parents may face is a lack of "know-how" to develop their child's literacy. Parents may want to spend more time providing their children with the building blocks for reading but be daunted by not knowing where to begin or what specific strategies they can employ. Feeling overwhelmed may lead them to put off spending time on reading even when they would like to do so. By providing concrete ideas for parents to implement, texting prompts can reduce the complexity of the task and increase parents' willingness to devote time to reading-related activities.

Stanford University researchers Benjamin York and Susanna Loeb evaluated the efficacy of an eight-month texting campaign for parents in the San Francisco Unified School District called READY4K! (York & Loeb, 2014). Every week, parents received three different types of texts related to early literacy. One of the texts conveyed a "fact" that was intended to engage parents and convey the benefits of early literacy, another text offered a "tip" for how the parent could promote early literacy with their child, and the final text conveyed a "growth" message to reinforce their efforts to promote reading for their children. Over the course of the eight months, the texts parents received emphasized progressively more sophisticated activities parents could do with their child. An early text might focus on parent-child conversations, while later texts provided parents with guidance on how to establish consistent reading routines with their child.

READY4K! was incredibly inexpensive to operate—less than $1 per family for the entire eight-month texting campaign. Its low costs belie its effectiveness, however. Parents who received the texts reported that they told more stories to their children, recited more nursery rhymes, and worked on more puzzles with their children than parents who were randomly assigned to receive biweekly texts with general information about the district. This increased engagement led to higher child scores on various early literacy measures.

A private company, Parent University, applied similar techniques in a texting campaign involving parents of children attending Head Start programs in the Chicago area (Ray, 2014). Parent University sent a randomly selected group of parents a series of texts that reminded them to engage in reading-related activities, along with concrete activities parents could try.

For instance, a text message to a parent of a three-year-old read, "Make ur own letter alphabet. Write the alphabet on paper. Cut out each letter & scramble on a table. Have your child put letters back in ABC order." The intervention is being studied by researchers at Northwestern University, and at the time of my writing a formal report was not available. According to a New America Foundation Ed Central blog post, however, parents in the treatment group reported being considerably more likely to engage in planned literacy-related activities such as reading to their child or telling stories (Ray, 2014).

Researchers have also used messaging prompts to provide parents of elementary, middle, and high school children with more information about how their child is performing in school. As the parent of a first grader who shares very little detail about what happens during her school day (aside from kickboxing class, which I hear about in all its splendor), I can personally attest to the lack of information that many parents have about their children's day-to-day performance. My daughter's academic trajectory is unlikely to suffer as a result of this lack of information, however. I know that her teacher and principal would be very responsive if I had any concerns, and my wife and I are fortunate that our work schedules allow us to spend a great deal of time with our children. Economically disadvantaged parents may not have the same opportunities with their children, because of longer and less standard work hours and/or because they have less confidence in reaching out to their child's school. As a consequence, parents are often unaware if their child has missed multiple assignments (Bergman, 2013). Parents may not realize until a report card arrives at the end of the term that their child is struggling.

This is another arena in which effectively delivered information can prompt parents to engage more actively with their child around schoolwork, in turn leading to improved performance. Economist Peter Bergman partnered with a school in a low-income area of Los Angeles to provide parents of sixth- through eleventh-grade students with detailed information about assignment completion and performance. Out of approximately 460 students in these grades, Bergman randomly selected just over 240 students' parents or guardians to receive almost weekly reports about students' missing assignments and grades. The information was highly specific to the student, providing detail down to the level of the name of the specific assignment or problem for which work was missing. Bergman also sent course grades to parents every five to eight weeks rather than at the end of the term so that parents could see how students' lack of assignment completion (or improved completion) affected course performance. Parents received messages through a variety of formats, including e-mails, phone calls, and text messages.

This information had substantial effects on parents' engagement with the school and in turn on students' work habits. Parents who received the informational prompts were more than 50 percent more likely to attend parent-teacher conferences than parents who did not receive the messages, while students whose parents received the messages were 25 percent more likely to complete assignments and 28 percent less likely to miss class. This combination of increased parental involvement and improved student work habits led, in turn, to substantial improvements in students' GPAs.

## TEXT MESSAGES TO MITIGATE SUMMER MELT

My own foray into applying insights from behavioral economics to address educational problems came in the form of an experiment along these lines. My colleagues and I set up a text messaging intervention to increase the share of college-bound, low-income high school graduates. In prior research with my colleagues Karen Arnold and Lindsay Page, we had documented that a substantial share of college-intending high school graduates fail to enroll anywhere in the year after high school as a result of financial needs and other obstacles they encountered during the summer months after graduation. These hurdles range from finalizing their financial aid and evaluating supplementary loan options to completing a host of paperwork and forms for freshman orientation, academic placement tests, and on-campus housing. In some urban districts, such as Boston, Massachusetts, and Fulton County, Georgia, 20 percent of college-bound students failed to matriculate. In other districts, such as Fort Worth, Texas, over 40 percent of students failed to follow through on their college intentions. Remember, these are kids who've already been admitted to a college. We refer to this phenomenon as "summer melt" (Castleman & Page, 2014).

At first glance, it may seem surprising that students who have already overcome so many hurdles—applying to college and for financial aid, graduating from high school—would falter in their college plans during the summer after high school. Yet, low-income students often have to juggle a variety of responsibilities over the summer—including summer employment and family responsibilities such as child care and translating for their parents—which can limit their focus on college tasks. At the same time that their attention is spread thin, students often confront complex and unanticipated tasks they need to complete in order to successfully enroll in their college. Many of these tasks relate to paying for college—from analyzing financial aid packages to completing loan applications, seeking loan counseling, evaluating tuition payment options, and even completing health insurance waiver forms.

As we've seen, limited attention and cognitively demanding tasks often lead people to put off important tasks. This response is particularly magnified for adolescents given their stage of cognitive development: the neural systems that respond to immediate stimuli, like spending time with friends, are fully developed, while the parts of adolescents' brains which govern judgment, deliberation, and planning are still in the nascent stages of development. All of these factors point to the importance of prompting students to complete tasks over the summer and providing them with adult assistance with more complex tasks related to financial literacy. And in fact, this is the role that many middle- and upper-income parents play with their children, pestering them to stay on top of tasks and in most cases taking charge of financial aid and tuition bills.

For low-income and first-generation college students, on the other hand, summer is a decidedly more challenging and nudge-free time period. High school counselors typically only work on ten-month contracts and so are unavailable. Students have yet to build relationships or engage with supports available at their college. Their parents may want to help but lack experience with college or financial aid. Isolated from professional support, students are not aware of the tasks required of them. Students lose out on financial aid for which they would have been eligible, and tuition bills wind up being higher than they had anticipated. Orientation or housing fees go unpaid, and as a result students miss orientation and cannot register for courses, or lose the opportunity to live on campus. Each of these responses can prevent students who have already accomplished so much and seem poised for collegiate success from following through on their postsecondary intentions.

One of the great tragedies in my mind is that the information about required summer tasks is often only a click away from the student. Chances are that the acceptance e-mail they received in March or April of senior year included a link to what they had to do over the summer—but many students don't read beyond the "Congratulations—you're accepted!" message at the top of the e-mail. Just about every college has an admitted students website describing these summer tasks, but many students have intermittent Internet access over the summer, and even with regular Internet access it doesn't occur to them to seek out this information. The mismatch between how colleges and students communicate illustrates the importance of effectively delivered communication. Sending information via e-mail or putting it on a website will rarely reach the very students whose educational access colleges are trying to promote.

Over the past several summers my colleagues and I have developed a text messaging intervention to get college-bound high school graduates to successfully matriculate at their intended school (Castleman & Page, 2015). We designed the messages to operate like behavioral multivitamins. Each week students receive a text message providing them with simplified and personalized information about a task they need to complete in order to enroll. The messages are personalized to each student's target college or university so that the information is highly relevant. Wherever possible, we include web links specific to each task in the messages so students can learn more or complete the task in the moment, before their attention is diverted elsewhere. And we make connecting to individualized advising and assistance as simple as responding to the text message. We have implemented this summer melt text messaging intervention in over a dozen school districts and with more than 10,000 students. The messaging campaign costs less than $10 per student but consistently leads to increased enrollment among students who lack access to other college-planning resources.

Unfortunately, just getting low-income students into college is not enough. Socioeconomic inequalities in college completion are pronounced and have only widened over time (Bailey & Dynarski, 2012). Nationally, a substantial share of college freshmen fail to make it to sophomore year, with retention rates particularly low among students at community colleges. For some of these students, the failure to persist is a result of insufficient academic performance or an inability to afford an additional year of college. But in other cases, informational and behavioral barriers may prevent students from continuing on in college. One prominent barrier that students encounter comes with renewing their financial aid. As we saw earlier, the FAFSA form is highly complex and is considered a primary barrier preventing college-ready low-income high school students from enrolling in college. While there have been a growing number of initiatives to provide high school seniors with more FAFSA completion support, there have been considerably fewer efforts to support college freshmen in renewing their aid, despite the fact that they have to complete the same complex form each year.

Currently, efforts to support FAFSA renewal are largely limited to e-mail reminders from the U.S. Department of Education, as well as from students' colleges and universities. Just as the information colleges send about required summer tasks may not be effectively delivered, these FAFSA renewal reminders may go unnoticed or overlooked. Even students who remember to renew their financial aid may struggle to allocate enough time or attention given their many academic, extracurricular, and social commitments. And student-to-advisor ratios sometimes exceed 1:1,000 at the postsecondary level, leaving students with little access to help with FAFSA renewal (Castleman, Schwartz, & Baum, 2015). Challenges with FAFSA completion are likely to be particularly pronounced at community colleges, where advising resources are often particularly limited and where students spend less time on campus, are more likely to be the first in their family to go to college, or are more likely to be burdened with work and family commitments (Bird & Castleman, 2014). Not surprisingly, 15–20 percent of freshman Pell Grant recipients in good academic standing fail to renew their FAFSA, even though these students stand to benefit the most and appear well poised for college success (Bird & Castleman, 2014). Failure to renew the FAFSA strongly correlates with failing to persist in college or earning a degree.

Lindsay Page and I designed another text messaging intervention to provide students with reminders and encouragement about FAFSA renewal. In partnership with uAspire, a Boston-headquartered nonprofit organization that provides college and financial aid advising, we sent college freshmen a series of text message reminders that provided students with information about resources at their own college or university where they could get help with financial aid. It also reminded students about important financial aid deadlines and offered students assistance from uAspire with filling out the FAFSA. As with our summer melt texting intervention, the intervention cost only several dollars per student but increased sophomore-year persistence among community college students by almost 20 percent (Castleman & Page, forthcoming).

## WHAT MAKES TEXT MESSAGING INTERVENTIONS SO SUCCESSFUL?

Several common trends unite my work and Peter Bergman's research on parental nudges and help identify why these strategies are so effective at leading students to make more informed educational decisions. First, we are able to capitalize on increasingly rich and available student-specific data to make the message content highly personalized—and therefore more salient. In Peter's case, he is able to rely on detailed assignment completion and other administrative data provided by his partner school. In the case of our work on summer melt, we relied on information about where students were planning to go to college which high schools collected from graduates during an exit survey.

Second, we relied on publicly available data to provide families with important information they may not have been aware of, had trouble understanding, or had not yet acted upon. Peter was able to relay to parents, for example, the teacher's expectations about an assignment, as well as actions students could take to stay on top of their classwork. Our summer melt texting project relied on information available on just about every college's "admitted students" web page. We took advantage of the fact that, in most urban districts, 80–90 percent of college-intending students plan to attend one of a small handful of colleges or universities. In some places, such as Albuquerque, 90 percent of college-going students attend one of two institutions: the University of New Mexico or Central New Mexico Community College. Across the several districts in which we worked, our research assistants were able to assemble all the college-specific tasks, due dates, and relevant web links in a matter of hours.

Third, our interventions relied on communications channels that reach young people and their families effectively. "Admitted students" web pages require students to (1) know they exist and (2) remember to seek them out. E-mails with information about required prematriculation tasks only work

if students (1) check their e-mails and (2) sift through all of the other messages clogging their in-boxes to find messages from their college. On the
other hand, each text message stands out as its own important content, at
least for a moment in time. The chirp or vibration that accompanies texts
we receive is also a powerful lure for our attention. Whatever else we are in
the middle of, most people will glance at their phone each time they get a
text. The ability of these alerts to capture our attention underlies why every
private company wants us to allow them to send push notifications when
we install their apps on our phone. They know they stand a much better
chance of selling us something if they can capture our attention with a chirp
from our phone. It's also why social media platforms like Facebook and
Twitter offer so many different ways of being notified when we receive a
new message. Even diehard Facebook users probably would log on less
often if keeping track of one's news feed required an active decision. Alerts
that our friends have posted a new photo, updated their status, tagged us
in photos, or mentioned us in a post are powerful draws to get back on the
site ourselves.

The confluence of these factors—rich, available student data, a trea-
sure trove of public information pertaining to education, and a wide range
of effective communications channels for reaching students and their
families—makes possible a wealth of behaviorally informed nudge interventions in education. My colleague Daphna Bassok at the University of
Virginia is exploring how to better convey information about child care center quality to help inform parents' decisions about where they enroll their
children in preschool. Along with several colleagues, I am working with
the College Board to send PSAT takers across the country text messages
with information about high-quality and affordable colleges they have a
good chance of being admitted to based on their PSAT score. In addition, I
am currently working with the Community College of Baltimore County to
send loan applicants personalized text messages to help them make more
informed borrowing decisions.

Of course, text messaging won't always be such an effective communications channel for reaching students. The more schools, nonprofit
organizations, and state agencies recognize the value of text as a means
of communication, the sooner this channel will get saturated like e-mail
did before it. For this reason, we need to stay at the frontier of how young

people and families communicate with each other. I often joke with my wife that my next innovation will be to develop a Snapchat or Instagram intervention (though I still haven't figured out the details). And just today, I learned about an organization that is using ads on a Pandora music station popular with teenagers to provide information about an educational program they offer. The organization told me that the response rates they have seen to these Pandora ads are far higher than other, more traditional outreach strategies. As this innovation illustrates, the only limit to our ability to communicate effectively with students is our own creativity.

## TURNING INTENTIONS INTO CONCRETE PLANS

The interventions I have described so far have relied on prompting people to take action on decisions they may not have known about or may have been putting off, on encouraging people to follow through on their intentions, and on using effective communications channels to provide people with information. Another strategy is to use prompts to help people make more concrete plans for how to follow through on important intentions (Rogers, Milkman, John, & Norton, forthcoming). One reason that planning prompts are effective is that they help people identify specific strategies for hurdles that may stand between them and a particular action. Take, for instance, scheduling a parent-teacher conference at your child's school (something I need to get around to doing!). Oftentimes these conferences happen on a day off from school or during an evening, which means that parents need to get time off of work and find someone to watch their children. Prompting people to reach out to a babysitter or block off time on their work calendar can help eliminate one of the logistical barriers that may stand in the way of the parent-teacher conference actually happening.

Another reason that planning prompts can positively influence whether people follow through on actions is that they help forge a cognitive link between the future event we want to follow through on (for example, attending the parent-teacher conference) and the action or behavior that we need to take (for example, finding a babysitter). If we make a plan to contact babysitters at a specific time and place—like when we get to work in the morning—we are more likely to remember to do so when we show up at our desk the next day (Rogers et al., forthcoming).

Despite the benefits of plan making, psychologists Todd Rogers, Katy Milkman, Leslie John, and Michael Norton note that many people often fail to create specific plans for important actions—and ironically, we are particularly likely to underplan when our intentions are strongest. As a result, sending people planning prompts can help them achieve intentions they have established for themselves or follow through on actions that they believe are important but which are not on the top of their mental priority list.

Planning prompts have generated positive effects in a range of fields, including voter mobilization, health care, and education. During the 2008 presidential election, for instance, psychologists David Nickerson and Todd Rogers (2010) divided over a quarter million registered voters in Pennsylvania into one of three experimental groups. A control group did not receive any outreach, while the first experimental group received a phone call reminding them of the upcoming election and encouraging them to vote. The second experimental group received the same phone outreach, and callers asked potential voters three additional plan-oriented questions: (1) when they would vote, (2) how they would travel to their polling place, and (3) where they would be coming from before they went to vote. Voters in the first experimental group were over two percentage points more likely to turn out to vote than voters in the control group. Voters who received the planning prompts were over four percentage points more likely to vote than the control group. Interestingly, the planning prompts were most effective for potential voters who lived by themselves and may therefore have been less likely to make a plan with a family member or roommate for when and how they would get to the poll.

Planning prompts have also been effective at encouraging people to follow through on important medical actions. Katy Milkman and colleagues worked with a company called Evive Health to send employees at a midwestern company mailings with reminders to get flu vaccinations (Milkman, Beshears, Choi, Laibson, & Madrian, 2011). Employees randomly assigned to a control group received personalized information about dates and times when they could get a flu vaccine at a nearby clinic. Employees assigned to get a planning prompt received the same letter, with one small addition: a box in which they were encouraged to write down the date and time for when they would get their vaccine. This minor nudge to make a plan for when employees would travel to the clinic increased vaccination rates by over 12 percent.

Not surprisingly, given adolescents' challenges with planning and organizations, planning prompts can also have beneficial impacts when used in a school setting. Psychologist Angela Duckworth and colleagues investigated whether encouraging high school sophomores to form "implementation intentions" for PSAT test prep improved students' performance (Duckworth, Grant, Loew, Oettingen, & Gollwitzer, 2011). As part of an end-of-year English assignment, students in the experiment were asked to write down two positive outcomes associated with completing practice PSAT test items, as well as two obstacles that could interfere with them completing the practice items. Students randomly assigned to a control group were then asked to write a brief essay about an influential person in their lives. Students in the treatment group were first asked to rewrite each positive outcome they associated with test preparation and the obstacle they could envision interfering with this preparation. Students were then asked to elaborate as much as possible on the positive outcomes and obstacles after "imagining it 'as vividly as possible'" (Duckworth et al., 2011, p. 21). This part of the experiment is referred to as "mental contrasting" and can also promote follow-through on goals they have established for themselves. Following the mental contrasting exercise, students in the treatment group were prompted to identify specific plans for how they would overcome each obstacle and also to indicate when and where they would complete a PSAT test booklet.

Upon receiving the PSAT test prep booklet over the summer, students who received the mental contrasting and implementation intentions intervention completed 60 percent more practice questions than students in the control group. Given the design of this experiment, it is not possible to separate out the unique effect of the implementation intentions from the mental contrasting, but the results lend support to the effectiveness of planning prompts on whether students follow through on their educational goals.

The opportunities to incorporate planning prompts in education are nearly limitless. Sending parents prompts to plan when they will review school choice materials could lead to more families selecting higher-quality schools for their children. Sending high school juniors prompts to plan when they will register for college entrance exams could lead to higher test taking and, as the studies we looked at in the previous chapter show, lead to improved college outcomes. Helping students make a plan for when they will seek out assistance with financial aid applications could increase the amount of aid they receive. Planning prompts could be equally beneficial for teachers, helping them set aside time to reach out to parents, or for administrators, helping them allocate more time for classroom observation and instructional support. These prompts could also be used to enhance many of the text message reminders I described earlier. For instance, the text messages to parents of young children could not only provide concrete preliteracy strategies but also encourage parents to identify a specific time each day when they would read to their child. Come to think of it, planning prompts might even help authors remember to block out additional time on their calendars to make further progress on the book they are striving to complete . . .

### HELPING PEOPLE COMMIT TO THEIR INTENTIONS

As we've seen, fairly simple prompts can lead to substantial improvements in whether people follow through on intentions and complete important tasks. A different way of helping people make active decisions is to provide opportunities for them to precommit to following through on intentions that are important to them. Take, for example, our choice of which television shows we watch (Read, Loewenstein, & Kalyanaraman, 1999).[4] If you asked me now, I would say that I'd really like to set aside time to watch one of the many Ken Burns PBS documentaries that have gotten so much acclaim. And if I had to precommit to the television shows I would watch over the next three weeks, there's a good chance one of the Burns films would be on the list. Left to the impulses of my present self, however, it's much more likely, when I plop down in front of the television after a long day of (trying) to write, that I'm going to binge watch *Game of Thrones*.

It turns out that many of us are (1) aware of our tendency to procrastinate and (2) willing to make commitments to bind us to future actions that we know we'd have trouble following through on when the moment for action eventually arrives. This is true of employees who want to save more for retirement, people who want to lose weight, and students who want to stay on top of their assignments.

As we know, employees do not always take the active steps necessary to enroll in their companies' retirement savings program, even when the company is offering them generous financial incentives to participate. This is despite the fact that most people want to save more for retirement. To help people follow through on this intention, economists Richard Thaler and Shlomo Benartzi (2004) designed an intervention called Save More Tomorrow through which employees could precommit to allocating a portion of future pay increases to retirement savings. Save More Tomorrow had several defining features. First, employees were approached about participating in the program well before an anticipated pay increase. After all, we tend to be more willing to forego present impulses in favor of future goals when this trade-off isn't something we actually have to face for some time. Second, the retirement contribution would kick in immediately after the pay raise, so that employees wouldn't feel they had gained a substantial increase in their present cash flow only to "lose" some of it to retirement savings a few paychecks later. Third, the retirement contribution rate would automatically increase with each scheduled pay raise, up to a maximum contribution rate that employees agreed to at the start of the program.

The authors piloted the Save More Tomorrow intervention with three companies working in different industries. The initiative was quite popular among employees, with nearly 80 percent of those offered the chance to participate signing up for the program. The substantial majority—80 percent—remained in the program over the forty-month duration of the intervention, and average retirement contribution rates increased from 3.5 percent with the first pay raise to 13.6 percent in the final pay raise. The ability to commit to retirement contributions ahead of future pay raises thus had a marked effect on whether employees were able to follow through on their savings goals.

A related idea, helping people form "commitment contracts" to achieve important goals, has gained traction recently, even leading to the creation of websites through which people can commit to follow through on intentions they have established for themselves—or pay a stiff price for failing to do so. One of these websites, Stickk, was created by Dean Karlan and colleagues. Karlan is an economist whose work inspired much of my thinking about how to use prompts to help students follow through on their college intentions.[5] Stickk allows anyone in the world to place bets on their own ability to meet a goal—exercising more, quitting smoking, calling their parents on a regular basis. Users can appoint a referee to oversee their progress and verify whether they are, in fact, sticking to their intentions. Karlan and colleagues encourage users to make the wager sufficiently painful—and even distasteful—that they will feel strong internal pressure to keep to their goal even when present impulses pull them in other directions. Gun control advocates, for instance, might promise to pay $1,000 to the National Rifle Association—something they would otherwise be loath to do—if they fail to follow through on their commitment to lose twenty pounds over a six-month period. Oh, and as an added incentive, these bets on Stickk are even public!

As a personal experiment, I recently made a commitment on Stickk to stop biting my nails. I've been doing it for as many of my thirty-seven years as I can remember, and it drives my family crazy. "Daddy!!" my daughter will shout when we're in the car, "PLEAAAAAASE stop biting your nails." I've had the embarrassing experience of getting irritated glances from concert goers when my biting is interrupting an orchestral performance, or having senior policy officials give me strange looks when I'm nibbling away during meetings at the White House. Of course, I know it's an awful habit, but I haven't been able to devote enough attention to making myself stop. So to put some skin in the game, I recently anted up $500 on Stickk to kick the habit. My wife (with undisguised glee) agreed to referee. If in six months I'm still biting my nails, I've agreed to send that $500 as a donation to the New York Yankees. As a lifelong New Englander and Red Sox fan,[6] I can't think of a worse way to spend my money. I encourage readers to search for me on Stickk and see whether I've kept to my commitment—and also to read many of the other fascinating wagers people have made to help them realize hard-sought goals.

Commitment devices like this can also promote better time management for students. To demonstrate this, psychologists Dan Ariely and Klaus Wertenbroch (2002) designed an experiment where they offered different due dates for course assignments to two sections of an executive education class at MIT. Students in each section had to complete three assignments over the course of the semester. In the control section, the authors assigned three evenly spaced and fixed deadlines for the assignments. In the experimental section, students were allowed to set their own deadlines. The only constraint was that students had to complete all assignments by the last day of class and had to stick to the deadlines they set for themselves. As the authors note, if procrastination wasn't a problem, students wouldn't impose any deadlines on themselves. Handing all assignments in by the last day would give them the most time to work on the assignments, as well as the opportunity to incorporate material from lectures later in the semester into their papers.

As it turns out, however, students in the class were very conscious of their tendency to procrastinate and set conservative deadlines for themselves. The average student in the experimental section set a due date for the first paper that was forty-two days before the end of the course and a due date for the second paper that was twenty-six days before the end of the term. Interestingly, students in the experimental group who on their own imposed evenly spaced deadlines scored similarly on their final grades to students in the control section who had evenly spaced deadlines imposed on them. By contrast, students whose deadlines were spaced less regularly throughout the term—perhaps too early, giving them less time to complete the assignment or less course material to incorporate, or too late, allowing too much work to pile up at the end—had end-of-course grades that were significantly *lower* than students in the control condition. These results suggest that while students recognize their tendency to procrastinate and believe that it is helpful to impose constraints that help them manage their time, they do not necessarily have a good understanding of *how* to enact these constraints effectively.

Commitment devices could be used at every level of education—even with preschoolers. My son Simon's teacher uses a form of commitment device to regulate the play sword fights that invariably break out on the playground. On the one hand, Simon and his buddies love to find sticks and pretend to be dueling ninjas. The challenge is that, in the moment, they're not very good about ensuring that sword swings only hit their friends' sticks and not their bodies. One approach would have been to ban all pretend sword fighting. But the kids aren't trying to hurt each other, and they have a lot of fun acting out their fantasies. Their teacher's solution was to have each child make a verbal commitment before they could pick up a stick: if, by accident, they hit a friend's hand or body during the sword fight, they would have to put their stick down and take a five-minute break. Much as they don't like being hurt, Simon and his friends especially don't like having to sit out while their friends are immersed in a ninja battle. Occasionally I get to watch the kids' sword fights at pick-up time, and it's pretty amazing to watch how carefully they now regulate their swings and adhere voluntarily—albeit reluctantly—to putting down their sticks if they do hit someone by accident.

For older students, commitment devices could take various forms. High school students who want to do better on assignments but who struggle to set aside enough time to work on them could be encouraged to identify something important to them (for example, the Snapchat app on their phone) that they would be willing to stake if they didn't complete a certain proportion of assignments on time each week. College students could stake access to preferred on-campus housing or better tickets at sporting events for the coming year on whether they completed a certain number of credits or maintained a certain GPA. For commitment devices to succeed, students (or the teachers and parents who work with them) need to (1) identify an action that a student is having trouble following through on, (2) set reasonable targets for improvement on this action, and (3) commit to voluntarily forego something that is important to them if they do not achieve their goals. Of course, this all requires some discipline—and the right prompts.

### FINDING THE RIGHT WAY TO FRAME INFORMATION

Next, let's consider the question of how the way information is framed can affect the choices people make. This idea often runs counter to our intuition. If you like brownies more than chocolate ice cream, you'll always choose the brownie when offered a choice between the two, right? What if you are offered brownies, chocolate ice cream, or vanilla ice cream? Even though brownies are still one of the options, in this scenario a surprising number of people change their choice to chocolate ice cream because there are now multiple ice cream options and people like chocolate more than vanilla (why people would ever choose vanilla over chocolate ice cream will forever baffle me).[7]

In education, students, parents, and teachers all respond differently depending on how information about performance or educational opportunities is framed. Economist Ignacio Martinez studied how students responded to question framing in the context of a massive open online course (MOOC) taught at the University of Virginia called "Foundations of Business Strategy." One of the course requirements students had to fulfill in order to receive a Statement of Accomplishment for the course was to complete six quizzes. The students could retake the quizzes as often as they wanted, with their best score being the quiz grade of record. As is often the case in MOOCs, only a small subset of the 64,415 students who initially enrolled in Foundations of Business Strategy completed the course assignments. Martinez assigned the 7,924 students who completed the first quiz to one of three experimental groups. One group served as a control and did not receive any outreach. Students in the second group received an e-mail stating the best grade they received on the first quiz. The e-mail then told them, "That means that you are doing *better* than XX percent of the class," where "XX percent" was customized to each student. The third group received the identical e-mail, except for the following change: "That means that you are doing *worse* than XX percent of the class."

This was the only e-mail Martinez sent students over the course of the MOOC. He then observed how likely students were to retake the first quiz, how likely they were to take subsequent quizzes, and how they performed on these quizzes. The single negatively framed e-mail led students who performed lower on the first quiz to exert more effort (measured, for instance, by the frequency with which they retook quizzes) and to perform higher on future quizzes. By contrast, the positively framed e-mail did not lead to significant increases in effort or performance (Martinez, 2013).

Researchers Matt Kraft and Todd Rogers (2014) investigated whether parents are more responsive to messages that highlight what their child is doing well or that emphasize where they need to improve. To explore this question, the authors sent parents weekly information about how their child was performing in summer school courses. As with Martinez's study, the researchers divided summer school enrollees into one of three groups. One group served as a control group. The second group of parents received weekly messages emphasizing what their child was doing well. The authors provide the following example of how a positive message might have been framed: "Kelly got an A– on her in-class quiz on cell biology—keep up the great work!" The third group received weekly messages emphasizing what their child needed to improve on in their summer classes. For instance,

"Tina missed two homework assignments this week—I know she can do better." At the end of the course, students whose parents received the messages about what they needed to improve on in the course were nearly ten percentage points more likely to earn course credit than students in the control group (Kraft & Rogers, 2014). The positively framed messages had a positive but not statistically significant effect relative to the control group on whether students earned credit.

One of the most important framing effects is whether a decision is framed as a loss or as a gain. It turns out that potential losses exert far more influence on people than potential gains of the same value or amount. My colleague Eileen Chou at the University of Virginia recently illustrated this principle through an on-campus blood drive. Chou and her colleague Keith Murnighan designed an awareness campaign to increase student participation in the blood drive (Chou & Murnighan, 2013). Two days prior to the event, the authors sent e-mails to over 3,500 undergraduates. Students in the control group received only time and location information for the blood drive. Another group of students was randomly selected to receive a message that emphasized that by donating blood, students would be saving lives: "Act now. Help save someone's life! Each year, 4.5 million Americans would die without blood transfusions. Every second, 2 people can be saved by donated blood. . . . Every pint that you donate can help them stay healthy. . . . Act now . . . help promote healthy lives." A third group received messages that emphasized instead that students' blood donation could prevent deaths from occurring: "Don't delay. Help prevent someone from dying! Each year, 4.5 million Americans would die without blood transfusions. Every second 2 people could die waiting for blood. . . . Every pint that you donate can help them avoid dying. . . . Don't delay . . . help prevent unnecessary deaths." While only a small portion of students who received the e-mails signed up for the blood drive, donation rates were significantly higher among students who received the "prevent death" message compared with students who received either the "save lives" or control group messages.

Economists Roland Fryer and Stephen Levitt examined whether the principle of loss aversion could be leveraged to increase the efficacy of teacher incentives (Fryer, Levitt, List, & Sadoff, 2012). Given the profound positive effect that teachers can have on their students' academic performance and longer-term success, policy makers have explored offering financial incentives as a strategy to motivate greater teacher effort and investment in their students. While teacher incentive programs have been piloted in a variety of districts across the country, relatively little is known about how to design incentives to most effectively challenge teachers to invest additional effort.

Fryer and Levitt offered kindergarten through eight-grade teachers in an urban school district the opportunity to participate in an incentive experiment where they would be rewarded with cash for their students' test score improvement over the coming academic year. One group of participating teachers received up-front cash payments. Teachers in this group had to return a portion of their payment if their students failed to meet a minimum threshold for growth over the coming year, but they also had the chance to earn additional payments if their students performed better than predicted. The other group of teachers was offered a more traditional incentive, where they would receive payments at the end of the year based on how much their students improved.[8] The amount teachers could earn was identical across both conditions; what differentiated the groups was that the first group of teachers stood to lose cash they already had in hand, while the second group of teachers had the potential to gain cash based on how their students performed over the course of the year. Students whose teachers were assigned to the "loss" group performed substantially higher relative to students whose teachers were in the "gain" group, both on the test that determined the size of teacher's payments and on state exams that were completely independent from the incentives.

Sometimes people's choices are influenced not only by the way new information is framed but also by the implicit conclusions they have drawn based on little bits of information that trickle in over time. Take, for instance, the issue of college costs. Sitting in an airport while I wrote this chapter, I asked five random people sitting near me to say the first word that comes to mind when they think about college costs. The responses were "crazy," "out of control," "skyrocketing," "way more than I can afford," and "heart attack." A pretty consistent pattern—but a well-informed assessment? Had these people recently looked up what college would cost them or their family members net of financial aid for which they might qualify? Probably not. My guess is that these reactions were driven much more by a steady stream of media headlines decrying soaring college tuitions. In fact, when I googled "skyrocketing tuition," the following three headlines were at the top of my search: (1) "How the Cost of College Went from Affordable to Sky-High" (NPR), (2) "Why Tuition Has Skyrocketed at State Schools" (New York Times), and (3) "The Facts behind Skyrocketing Tuition" (Daily Kos). Stories like these invariably cite annual tuition and room and board costs at places like Harvard, where they now exceed $60,000 per year. When people hear stories like this over and over again, it tends to form a mental anchor for how they think about college costs. When it comes time to think about applying to college, these anchors can lead some people to preemptively conclude, "I can't afford college," when in fact many people pay a substantially lower net price once financial aid is applied to their tuition bill. While numbers are particularly weighty anchors, other pervasive narratives can also influence people's educational decisions. For instance, hearing repeated stories about "struggling public schools" and "the narrowing of school curricula" may lead some families to pursue private options even if their local school is in fact doing quite well and has a creative and broad curriculum.

Knowledge is power, as they say, and providing families with better information has the potential to help them make more active and informed educational decisions. But as we've seen, just making information available is not enough. Educators need to think carefully about how information is framed and delivered. Even with digestible information at their fingertips, people may still struggle to make decisions when immediate demands interfere with their ability to follow through on longer-term intentions. Providing prompts, planning guidance, and commitment devices can help people better align their present actions with future goals. From a policy perspective, there is tremendous promise in these approaches because they are often very affordable, scalable to large populations, and quite effective.

So far I have discussed decision making in education primarily from the perspective of how individual students and their families evaluate the various options available to them. But our decisions are not made in isolation from the social contexts that surround us. What we perceive others to expect of us, the way people respond to our actions and behaviors, the choices we observe our peers making, and the way we perceive social norms all influence our own decisions in education. Next, we'll explore these social influences on decision making in greater detail.

## Chapter 4

Following Our
Friends — or Not

MY CAREER IN EDUCATION began as a teacher and then school administrator at the Met Center, a network of small public high schools in Providence, Rhode Island. The Met serves primarily low-income students of color, many of whom would be the first in their family to go to college. The school's organization and curriculum were about as innovative as you could imagine within the limits of urban public education. The entire school was built around personalized, real-world learning. Starting in ninth grade, students spent two days a week at an internship in the community connected to their personal interests. To give you an example, one of my students was obsessed with sharks. There aren't a lot of professional shark chasers in Rhode Island, so instead we got him an internship at a pet store. But he worked his way up from there and for the next two years interned at the Rhode Island fish hatchery. By senior year he was taking the train into Boston twice a week to intern at the aquarium, where he finally got to live his dream of feeding and caring for sharks.

Students entered school as part of fifteen-student advisories or groups in which they remained for the next four years. Advisors, or teachers like me, were responsible for helping students find internships and develop internship projects through which they could learn academic concepts in applied settings. As you can imagine, students grew incredibly close with their advisory mates and with their advisor over the four years. Many felt by the end of high school that the advisory had become their second family.

The school scored incredibly well on various measures: our graduation rates exceeded 95 percent, we consistently scored at the top of the state on survey measures of student and parent satisfaction, and we had very few instances of violence or theft despite being located in one of the roughest neighborhoods in Providence. But this was the early 2000s, when test-based accountability was starting to ramp up across the country, and our school was evaluated by the state in large part based on how our students performed on tenth-grade math and English language arts assessments. The challenge, of course, was that we didn't have conventional math or English classes—or any classes at all, for that matter. Our students' academic learning was entirely through what they learned at their internships and through their projects, as well as through whatever advisors taught during group advisory time at the beginning and end of each day. We knew that our students were bright, hardworking, and passionate about their learning, but we also needed them to score well enough on the state assessments so we would be allowed to stick to our pedagogy.

On the first day of testing each year, we would organize a morning meeting with all the tenth graders. We served a hot breakfast—pancakes, eggs, sausage, the whole nine yards—and then gave a pep talk. We were frank and up-front with the students: we described the political climate around test-based accountability and let them know that if they performed well on the tests, it would provide running room for us to keep the school squarely focused on authentic, individualized learning—not only for them but also for their younger brothers, sisters, and cousins who might attend the Met in the future. In other words, we wanted them to understand the stakes of these standardized tests. We knew that many of our students were nervous about the tests, having had relatively little formal instruction over the past two and a half years, and we encouraged them to try their best on the test. "Even if you haven't sat through algebra and English literature classes," we told them, "you've developed other valuable skills at your internships like creativity, problem-solving, and perseverance that can help you get to the bottom of what each question is asking."

This pep talk was always well received. Our tenth graders were mature enough to grasp the political realities and to feel a sense of responsibility to ensure that younger students had the same opportunities from which they had benefited. They also understood that skills they had developed in one setting could be transferred to other contexts. We were probably the only school in the state where a motivational speech about state exams was met with an enthusiastic round of applause.

I can't say whether our pep talk had any unique effect on students' test performance (this was before my research training; otherwise, it might have occurred to me to randomly assign students to either hear this speech or just go right into taking the test). Our students certainly didn't score in the top ranks of the state—those slots were dominated every year by the most affluent communities in Rhode Island. But despite not offering formal math or English language arts instruction, our students performed on par each year with the other public schools in Providence.

Implicit in our approach was the belief that tests don't objectively measure what students know. Rather, they assess some combination of knowledge and effort. If we could motivate students to try harder, we speculated, they would do better on the tests. A corollary to this view—and the reason we gave this speech every year—is that various factors might impede students from trying their hardest. The state tests had little meaning for their own lives (at the time the tests had no bearing on whether students graduated from high school). Students might have lacked confidence in their own ability to perform well on tests, especially having participated in such an unconventional education. Or, they may have felt that no one expected students from "an alternative school" to do well on tests that were assessing proficiency in traditional academic domains.

We didn't know it at the time, but the rationale behind our pep talk aligned with important psychological theories about how students perform in social contexts. Decades of research have demonstrated that students' performance—whether in middle school, high school, or college—can be profoundly affected by what they perceive society to expect of students "like them" or by their beliefs about whether they belong in educational environments that have traditionally been dominated by certain ethnic and socioeconomic groups. Students' performance can also be influenced by their views and beliefs about their own potential for learning and success. I organize this chapter around these core theories, providing an intuitive overview of each, along with examples of how they have informed the design of psychologically informed interventions to improve student achievement.

Before looking at our first idea, *stereotype threat*, it is worth noting that this research has its roots primarily in social psychology rather than behavioral economics. But behavioral economics largely operates at the intersection of economics and psychology. Given the overarching focus of this book on how to help students and families make informed decisions in education, these theories merit close attention because they show how students respond to the way that information is presented. The cases I highlight below also share a common feature with those highlighted in earlier chapters: they are typically low-cost and scalable solutions to improve student success and address long-standing inequalities in education.

## STEREOTYPE THREAT

Each of us can probably think about a negative stereotype that applies to some aspect of our identity. I am Jewish, and as a kid I was always aware of the stereotype that, Sandy Koufax aside, Jews aren't very athletic. This awareness didn't affect how I did academically or how I interacted with my friends, but it was definitely on my mind during any kind of sports practice. I grew up as one of only a small handful of Jewish kids in a town that was obsessed with sports. Our high school teams were routinely state champions in football and soccer, and the varsity athletes were lionized like Greek gods. Think *Friday Night Lights* (the television version), except in shoreline Connecticut.

I was always one of the slowest and least coordinated kids on every team, whether soccer, baseball, or basketball. I distinctly remember being preoccupied with whether I was going to hear some crack about the "fat Jew" lumbering up and down the field or around the bases (this actually happened a few times). Now, my athletic ineptitude was probably mainly due to genetics, but this preoccupation certainly didn't help.

Thanks to pioneering work by psychologists Claude Steele and Josh Aronson (1995), we have come to recognize that this anxiety about confirming negative stereotypes about one's group—or the experience of stereotype threat, as the authors call it—can have negative and lasting effects on performance in many ways. We don't need to believe negative stereotypes to be affected by them. The awareness that particular stereotypes exist and the desire to not confirm these beliefs through our own behavior can impose substantial cognitive and emotional burdens on people. In the short term these burdens translate into heightened anxiety, which reduces our performance on the task at hand. In the longer term stereotype threat can lead us to disassociate from activities that are negatively stereotyped with our group. In my case, negative stereotypes about Jews and athletics generated anxiety for me during every sports practice and over time led me to give up organized sports in favor of domains where I was more successful, like the classroom.

Steele and Aronson's work focused on how stereotype threat can contribute to persistent academic achievement gaps between Black and White students. The authors designed an experiment in which Black and White college students were asked to complete a portion of the verbal Graduate Record Examination (GRE)—the test that many college graduates take as part of their application to graduate school. One group of students was told that the test was diagnostic of their intellectual ability, while the control group was told that the test was simply a lab-based problem-solving activity and was not diagnostic of their underlying ability. Black and White students performed equally well in the latter group. But for the students who were told that the test was diagnostic of their ability, Blacks performed substantially lower than both White students in the same group and their Black counterparts in the control group. Concerns about confirming negative stereotypes about Blacks' intelligence generated anxiety and self-doubt for these students, contributing to their diminished performance.

In another version of the experiment, all participants were told that the test was not diagnostic of their ability. Some students were randomly assigned to list their race before taking the exam, while others were not. Black students who were primed to identify their race performed substantially lower than Blacks who were not primed to indicate their race. Even though subjects were told that the test was not a measure of their intellectual ability, the explicit connection between race and an academic assessment led to a sense of stereotype threat and, in turn, reduced performance.

Steele and Aronson's groundbreaking work focused on race—and more specifically whether students were Black or White—as a differentiating characteristic for whether students experienced stereotype threat in an academic setting. Many of us, however, identify several salient characteristics as essential to our identity: gender, class, religion, sexual orientation, to name a few. Subsequent work has demonstrated how stereotype threat can operate differently for people depending on which aspect of their identity is primed. In one study, for instance, Asian American women were assigned to take a math test. For these individuals, two countervailing stereotypes were at play: Asian Americans are often stereotyped to perform well in math, while females are often stereotyped to have less mathematic aptitude than males (Shih, Pittinsky, & Trahan, 2006). Prior to taking the math test, the Asian American women were divided into three groups. The first group was primed to indicate their race, while the second group was asked to indicate their gender. A third group served as a control and was not primed to indicate any social identity. Participants who were primed to think of themselves as Asian performed substantially better than the control group, while participants who were asked to think of themselves as female performed substantially worse than the control.

An important insight from this research is that students' academic performance can be influenced by making different aspects of their identity more or less salient during tests. This is not to suggest that educators should exploit existing stereotypes (for example, priming Asian students to think about their race when taking math tests). One strategy is, in fact, to do the opposite—to de-emphasize group membership that may elicit a sense of stereotype threat among students. In one study, for instance, researchers simply moved questions about race/ethnicity and gender to the end of the AP Calculus exam rather than ask these questions at the beginning. The authors found suggestive evidence that this simple change increased performance among female students taking the exam (Stricker & Ward, 2004, as cited in Danaher & Crandall, 2008).[1]

Another strategy is to buffer against the effects of stereotype threat by encouraging students to think about characteristics that set themselves apart as individuals but which are not directly tied to their social identity (Ambady, Paik, Steele, Owen-Smith, & Mitchell, 2004). In one study, women were first assigned to two groups: the first was primed to think of themselves as female, while the second was not. Students were then randomly assigned to an exercise that prompted them to think about their individually defining characteristics or to a control group. Students in the "individuation" group were asked to list things like their favorite book and movie, as well as their three best and worst qualities. As in the study cited above, students who were primed to think just of their gender performed worse than students who did not receive this prime. But students who received the gender prime and the individuation exercise performed just as well as students who were not prompted to think about their gender.

One reason that "individuation"-type activities may be important is that different aspects of people's identities (gender, race, ethnicity, and so on) may be front-of-mind during assessments regardless of whether people have been primed to think of these identities (for example, by demographic questions at the start of the exam). Encouraging students to think about individual traits can therefore help draw students' attention away from anxieties associated with some aspect of their social identity.[2]

Priming students to think about positive aspects of their identity can also mitigate stereotype threat and reduce achievement gaps in education. Working in a racially diverse middle school in the Northeast, researchers randomly assigned a group of seventh-grade students to participate in a self-affirmation exercise (Cohen, Garcia, Purdie-Vaughn, Apfel, & Brzustoski, 2009). Students in the treatment group were given several brief writing assignments during the year, in which they were asked to reflect on an important personal value. These values didn't have to be academic— students could write about their athletic ability, the importance of family, or their love of music. Students assigned to the control group were asked to write instead about something other people might value about them but that they didn't personally value in themselves. White students who participated in this intervention were unaffected, either in terms of achievement or in their beliefs about their own potential for success. For Black students, and particularly lower-performing Black students, on the other hand, the impacts were pronounced. Two years after the end of the intervention, students who participated in the self-affirmation exercise had GPAs that were anywhere from 0.25 to 0.40 points higher than students who did not participate. The authors argue that the positive and lasting effects of this experiment can be attributed to the positive cycle that the writing activity promoted: encouraging them to affirm their own value led students to engage more in school, which promoted a stronger sense of belonging and potential for academic success. These positive self-perceptions helped buffer stereotype threat and contributed to stronger academic outcomes.

This strategy of priming students to think about aspects of their identity which are associated with academic success has gained considerable traction. In November 2013, Michelle Obama gave a speech to high school sophomores at the Bell Multicultural High School in Washington, DC. The school serves primarily students of color from economically disadvantaged

neighborhoods in the District. Rather than see the challenges they encountered on a daily basis as an impediment to their educational success, Mrs.
Obama encouraged students to view these experiences as assets on the
pathway to college:

> Maybe you've had problems at home and you've had to step up, take
> on extra responsibilities for your family. Maybe you come from a tough
> neighborhood, and you've been surrounded by things like violence
> and drugs. Maybe one of your parents has lost a job and you've had to
> struggle just to make it here today.
>
> One of the most important things you all must understand about
> yourselves is that those experiences are not weaknesses. They're not
> something to be ashamed of. Experiences like those can make you
> stronger and more determined. They can teach you all kinds of skills
> that you could never learn in a classroom—the skills that will lead you
> to success anywhere in life (White House, 2013).

The First Lady went on to encourage students to leverage these skills toward furthering their education by actively engaging in classes, completing their homework, and—most importantly in my mind—continuing to
invest effort even in the face of repeated challenges.

The opportunities to apply positive identity priming in education are
nearly limitless. Many of the examples I highlight above focused on priming students to perform well on tests and other assessments. But similar
techniques could be leveraged before other important action points. For
instance, the "individuation" exercises described above could be leveraged
to encourage more young girls to consider signing up for enrichment programs or summer learning experiences in science- and math-related fields.
Priming students to think about the ways they support their families and
neighborhoods—and how they are supported by their communities—might
contribute to greater engagement in group projects at school or heightened
willingness to participate in community projects. Having students reflect on
the adult mentors with whom they are most comfortable talking could help
them feel more at ease during college or internship interviews. We all have
aspects of our identities which are a source of confidence and esteem and
other aspects that, in certain contexts and settings, can generate consider-

able anxiety. By helping students focus on the positive aspects of their identity, educators can remove obstacles that can otherwise prevent students from demonstrating how much they have learned or from achieving their full educational potential.

## SOCIAL BELONGING

In the introduction I described Vince, one of my students at the Met whose college search was initially limited to two institutions: the University of Miami, whose football team impressed him, and Harvard University, whose brand name is as ubiquitous as Coca-Cola or M&M's. For Vince, a lack of family experience with a fuller set of college options limited his awareness of what schools might be better matches for his abilities and interests—and where he had a much better chance of being admitted and actually succeeding. But the student whose college-going experience stands out most in my mind is Paul. Paul arrived at the Met before his junior year, having recently emigrated from a Latin American country. Paul grew up in circumstances no child should have to endure: crushing poverty, pervasive gang violence, family neglect and abuse. When he arrived, Paul barely spoke any English and was very self-conscious about speaking in front of the other students in his advisory.

Paul struggled for months to find an internship. He didn't have a clear sense of which interests he wanted to pursue, and he was very anxious about having to schedule an interview with potential mentors. Paul's English steadily improved as his junior year progressed, and it was clear that he was very bright and inquisitive—but halfway through the first semester, he still hadn't developed any promising internship leads.

One day Paul was out with his adopted mother and happened to walk by a photographer's studio in Providence. The photographer specialized in landscape photographs, and his storefront window featured dazzling images from the Rhode Island landscape: stunning fall foliage, yachts sailing into the sunset on Narragansett Bay. Paul turned to his mother and said, "Maybe I could do that for an internship?"

Several months later, Paul was headlong into a landscape photography internship. Most students' internship hours aligned with the school day, but Paul's schedule worked around the quality of the light: sunrises over the bay, a particularly crisp blue sky in Roger Williams Park, a breathtaking sunset over the city skyline. Paul, we soon discovered, had an incredible eye for photography and a subtle touch with the camera. The images he'd capture in one week of work rivaled the portfolios of seasoned landscape photographers. Paul's mentor helped him matte and frame his pictures, and he was soon making a steady business selling them.

When it came time to apply for college, Paul's photography also caught the eye of many admissions offices, including a prestigious college of art and design. Not only was Paul admitted to this college, but he was offered a very generous financial aid package. Combined with local scholarship funds he could access, Paul would be able to enroll in the college on a full ride. In two years he had come as far as any student possibly could, from daily violence and poverty in Mexico to one of the best art and design colleges in the country, where he would be able to pursue his passion for photography.

However, when it came time to send in a financial deposit in May of senior year, Paul decided that he wasn't going to enroll. I was caught completely off guard. This was the first I had heard of any reluctance on his part. Initially, Paul explained his decision as a function of wanting to pursue his photography business full-time. But over hours and days of discussing what he would do, a deeper story emerged. "There's no one there like me," Paul said. "No one who looks like me, no one who sounds like me." From the outside we were all focused on how much Paul had achieved in two short years. For Paul, however, what stood out most was how different he still felt from the other students around him—and particularly from the students he met when he visited the art and design college. Try as we might—me, his mentor, other staff at the school—we couldn't persuade Paul to give the college a try. The prospect of feeling out of place was just too daunting for him.

Paul is not alone in wondering whether he belonged on a college campus or in worrying about how he would adjust to collegiate life. The college transition is challenging for many students—something I observed firsthand in my years as a residential advisor at Harvard. Especially at more selective schools, students have to grapple with the shift from being the big fish in a small pond at their high school to swimming with many talented fish at their college. They wrestle with balancing academic, extracurricular, and social commitments and with staying on top of their coursework when their days have so much less structure and external direction.

But for students from college-educated and more affluent families, concerns about the college transition typically do not cause them to question whether they should enroll. If anything, the freedom, independence, and novelty of college are what excite students most about freshman year (more so, I dare say, than their expository writing or calculus courses).

Years of research have demonstrated that it is common for underrepresented students to have doubts about whether they will develop a sense of community at college—and furthermore, that these doubts can impede students from enrolling in college or succeeding once they are there (Walton & Cohen, 2011). Some students view college campuses as the exclusive domain of rich, privileged (and usually White) students. Others worry that they would be one of only a handful of students of color on campus (Walton & Cohen, 2007). Students may feel that in order to succeed in college, they have to downplay or sacrifice entirely group identities that are important to them (Cohen & Garcia, 2005). For many students, the uncertainty they face about fitting in is compounded by having never actually set foot on campus before it comes time to enroll. Time and travel costs may make it difficult for students to visit their colleges during the application season. At an even more basic level, first-generation college students—particularly those who received little college counseling in high school—may struggle to imagine the academic and social dimensions of college life. As it did for Paul, this uncertainty about fitting it can generate considerable anxiety, potentially leading them to forego their plans (Lovelace & Rosen, 1996). Doubts about social belonging can lead students to interpret challenges they encounter in the first semesters of college as proof that they can't succeed in higher education, rather than viewing these hurdles as a normal part of the transition to a new environment (Walton & Cohen, 2011).

## SOCIAL NORMS, UNCERTAINTY, AND DECISION MAKING

Now, step back and think about how you make decisions when confronted with uncertainty. Let's say you just moved to a new city and you're trying to find a good auto mechanic. If you're like most people, you do one of two things: (1) you ask people at work or in your neighborhood which mechanic they use, or, increasingly, (2) you look on social review sites like Yelp or Angie's List. You might be particularly influenced by the recommendations of people who have the same car brand as you or who have run into the same kind of car trouble as you.

In uncertain situations, most of us are influenced by what we perceive to be the social norms, and we're particularly likely to follow the lead of peers we perceive to be most similar to us (Cialdini, 2001; White, Hogg, & Terry, 2002). Private sector companies recognize this—it's why Amazon tells us what other people bought when we are having a hard time choosing which book to read or which Star Wars LEGO set our kids are most likely to enjoy. One of my favorite examples of this power of social norms has to do with not education, or even public policy, but rather . . . hotel towels. Psychologists Noah Goldstein, Robert Cialdini, and Vladas Griskevicius (2008) designed an experiment in which they modified the "hang up your towel and save the environment" cards that are now ubiquitous in most hotel rooms. One group of guests at a hotel was randomly assigned to receive a standard environmental message. Another group received a card that informed them that most guests at the hotel reused their towels. A third group received a card that said that most prior guests in their room reused their towels. The social norm information provided to the second group led to higher towel reuse rates than in the group that received the standard environmental message. What I find particularly fascinating is that guests who were told about the towel-hanging habits of prior occupants of their room were the most likely to reuse their towels. They, of course, had no idea *who* had actually stayed in the room before them, but the social norm about their room felt more proximal to them than the social norm about the entire hotel and led to more environmentally friendly behaviors.

Researchers have designed a range of interventions that leverage the power of peer norms to help improve students' behaviors in education. One approach has been to use peer mentors to help students through challenging educational transitions they encounter. Peer mentor outreach is one strategy my colleagues and I have investigated to help college-bound graduates successfully transition to college. As we saw earlier, students encounter an array of complex financial and procedural tasks to complete during the summer after high school, at a time when they typically lack much professional support. The challenge of completing these tasks may exacerbate misgivings about belonging in college which Paul and many other students experience in the months before they are slated to matriculate, and can lead some students to throw in the towel (Castleman & Page, 2014). Peer mentors who graduated from the same communities and went on to thrive in college can offer invaluable perspectives on how they navigated and overcame similar challenges during the summer months. The similarity of their experiences is likely to make the advice and encouragement they offer particularly salient for recent high school graduates.

To investigate this hypothesis, we randomly assigned college-intending students in three Massachusetts cities and in Philadelphia to receive proactive peer mentor outreach during the summer after high school graduation. Peer mentors worked to build relationships with students, to assess their readiness for college, and to connect them to professional advising support when they encountered challenging financial or procedural hurdles. In most cities, 50–60 percent of students wound up meeting with a peer mentor, and these interactions led to substantial increases in the rate of students who successfully enrolled at four-year colleges and universities in the semester immediately after high school (Castleman & Page, 2015). Other researchers have found similar success pairing high school seniors with college mentors to help them complete college and financial aid applications (Bos, Berman, Kane, & Tseng, 2012; Carrell & Sacerdote, 2013).

Mentoring programs have also had a positive influence on students' decisions and behaviors at other educational stages. Big Brothers / Big Sisters is one of the better-known mentoring programs in the country, serving over a quarter million kids each year. The program pairs young, well-educated adults with youth from primarily low-income, single-parent households. The mentor pairs typically meet three to four times a month, with some relationships lasting several years, and pursue activities of shared interest. Mentor pairs might play sports, study at the library, or cook meals together.

In the early 1990s, researchers Jean Grossman and Joseph Tierney (1998) conducted an experimental evaluation of the Big Brothers / Big Sisters program. Youth in eight large cities in the United States were randomly assigned either to be paired with a mentor or to a program waitlist. The authors then tracked students' outcomes for the next eighteen months. While the researchers were not able to obtain administrative data to directly observe changes in students' behavior, there were substantial differences in students' self-reports between the treatment and control groups. Students whom Big Brothers / Big Sisters tried to pair with a mentor were substantially less likely to report using illegal drugs or alcohol or to report being violent toward another person. They also reported skipping half as many days of school as students in the control group. These partnerships clearly have a positive effect on the students.

### LOWER-TOUCH INTERVENTIONS TO PROMOTE A SENSE OF SOCIAL BELONGING

While establishing mentoring relationships is likely beneficial at many stages in students' education, it is also possible to impart positive peer norms—and to create lasting impacts on students' success—through considerably lower touch interventions. Much of the pioneering work to promote a stronger sense of social belonging among disadvantaged students has been conducted during the high school–to–college transition. A landmark study by psychologists Greg Walton and Geoffrey Cohen (2011) involved college freshmen at Stanford University. Stanford is home to some of the smartest and most accomplished students in the country, but it, too, faces academic achievement gaps between White and Black students. The authors designed an intervention to investigate whether promoting a greater sense of social belonging among Black students would contribute to greater resilience in the face of challenges they encountered on campus and, as a result, improved academic achievement relative to their White peers.

Students in the treatment group were asked to read a report that purportedly provided feedback from a campus survey of upperclassmen. In the report, the upper-class students described how they had experienced difficulty transitioning to Stanford during their freshman year, but over time they developed a sense of community and strong friendships and felt much better about their Stanford experience than they initially did. After reading this report, treatment group students were asked to write an essay about their own challenges transitioning to college and to craft this essay as a speech they could give to future students to bolster their confidence during their own transition. The entire process took one hour to complete.

The authors tracked outcomes for both these students and students randomly assigned to a control group over the next several years. The combined strategy of sharing narratives of older students describing their own challenges and providing students with the opportunity to relay this messaging to younger students in their own words helped foster greater resilience among Black freshmen, allowing them to persevere through the remainder of their time at Stanford. Black students who received the social belonging intervention reported a greater sense of connection and less self-doubt, as well as greater health and happiness, than Black students in the control group. By graduation, the GPA gap between Black and White students had been cut in half, and the share of Black students graduating in the top 25 percent of their class increased threefold.

Psychologists Nicole Stephens, Maryam Hamedani, and Mesmin Destin (2014) designed a similar intervention to promote a stronger sense of social belonging among college freshmen at Northwestern University. The authors' study differed in two important ways from the Walton and Cohen experiment. First, Stephens and colleagues targeted first-generation college students rather than underrepresented minority students. Second, rather than have students read narrative reports from upperclassmen, the authors had the freshmen participate in workshops led by upperclassmen. In the panels attended by students in the control group, upper-class students talked about their transition to college and how they each found success on campus. Students assigned to the treatment group participated in panels where upper-class students talked explicitly in terms of how their social class background influenced their transition and how these backgrounds led to different transitional experiences from other students on campus. The authors theorized that making these differences transparent would help students understand *why* they struggled more in the transition to college, and why it was sometimes necessary for them to seek out support that their peers might not need (for example, first-generation students might need additional advising about course selection if their parents did not feel confident providing guidance). After participating in the panel, students recorded a video essay in which they explained what they had learned and offered advice to future college freshmen.

The results of this intervention were equally impressive. While first-generation students in the control group were substantially less likely to seek out college-based supports than students from college-educated families, there was no such gap among students who participated in the difference-education treatment. By the end of freshman year, the GPA achievement gap between first-generation students and students from college-educated families had declined by 63 percent.

One question readers may have about this work is whether these interventions are as effective outside of the context of highly selective colleges and universities. While I view this as an important and open question for further investigation, early evidence suggests that social belonging interventions can also be quite effective when conducted from the high school side. In one study involving students from a charter school who had been admitted to college, students who were randomly assigned to participate in a forty-five-minute social belonging session at the end of senior year were 34 percent more likely to be enrolled in college full-time during the year after high school (Logel, Murphy, Walton, & Yeager, 2011).

What I find particularly exciting is the potential scalability of these interventions. Greg Walton, David Yeager, and a team of researchers at Stanford and other universities are currently developing versions of the social belonging intervention which can be administered online to large volumes of students (Logel et al., 2011). Think about a principal or school counselor sending a message (via text, not e-mail) to their students which includes a link to a YouTube video on social belonging at college. Just as in the interventions described above, the students could read a narrative or watch a video of current college students talking about their own adjustment to campus life and could be prompted to write encouraging messages for younger students. These types of activity could be done with tens or hundreds of thousands of students each year—though it's worth noting that Walton, Yeager, and colleagues emphasize the importance of making the narratives as relevant to the local context as possible, down to the level of the accents of the students featured on a video clip.

While much of the work on social belonging has focused on the high school–to–college transition, these strategies could be applied at other important stages in students' lives. In communities that have pursued aggressive school choice policies, for instance, a substantial share of students transition to schools outside of their neighborhoods, and potentially apart from their peer groups. These students may have similar doubts about belonging and might benefit from reading about how other students had navigated the transition to a new school environment. Social belonging interventions could be piloted with parents of preschool-age children who are thinking about sending their child to a new early education setting. Hearing how similar families had made the transition to a new day care setting might increase parents' willingness to place their child in a different care setting. Within schools, social belonging interventions could be used to help students adjust to more rigorous coursework, especially in schools where academic tracking remains fairly segregated along racial/ethnic or socioeconomic lines.

## GROWTH MINDSETS

My seven-year-old daughter is going to be either a lawyer or a rabbi. She went to a Jewish kindergarten last year and continues to go to religious school every Sunday. Learning about Jewish morals, history, and traditions has instilled in her a strong appreciation for the law—and she has made it her business to create several guiding rules for our family. Among them:

- Castlemans keep their promises.
- Castlemans don't lie.
- Castlemans don't say "hate" or "stupid."

You can imagine her joy upon learning of the *actual* Ten Commandments.

My favorite of her laws, and one that I throw back at her on a regular basis, is this:

- Castlemans don't quit.

As a parent, I've gotten a lot of mileage out of this maxim—when Lila was first learning to read, when she wanted to bike up a particularly steep hill behind our house, when she's practicing violin. There was a time during each of these events when Lila got frustrated and wanted to give up. All I had to say was, "What's the Castleman rule?" To her credit, she doesn't just make the laws; she also follows them. And more importantly, I've noticed that she's starting to internalize that if she keeps working at something, she'll steadily get better and better. She's recognized that reading practice has allowed her to read *Magic Tree House* books on her own, that repeated practice has helped her crest the steep hill on her bike, and that lots of practice on the violin . . . well, that's still a work in progress. I, too, have learned to praise her effort, rather than what she accomplishes. For this I have Carol Dweck to thank.

Dweck is a social psychologist who has spent much of her career studying how people respond when faced with challenges. Some people have what Dweck refers to as a "growth" mindset (Dweck, 2006). These individuals believe that skills and intelligence are malleable and can be improved with hard work, practice, and sustained effort. People with a growth mindset tend to persevere through challenges they encounter, since doing so may help them develop new skills. Other people have what Dweck refers to as a "fixed" mindset. These individuals tend to view ability as a fixed entity—you're either smart or you're not; you're either a talented athlete or you're not. As a result, when people with a fixed mindset encounter challenges, they tend to view this as an indication that they inherently lack the necessary skills—whether academic, athletic, or otherwise—to succeed.

Over repeated studies, Dweck and her colleagues find that (1) fixed and growth mindsets are established early in life; (2) people with growth mindsets tend to be better at overcoming challenges and succeeding academically; and (3) even for youth who do not initially have a growth mindset, it is possible to promote one through low-touch, psychologically informed interventions.

The way that parents and teachers provide feedback to children at an early age can influence the type of mindset they develop. To illustrate this point, Dweck and colleague Melissa Kamins randomly assigned groups of kindergarteners to hear different types of feedback given after a child in a story completed a task (Kamins & Dweck, 1999). In one story, for instance, a child tried hard to stack blocks neatly, but the stack still looked messy after the task was completed. Groups of children then heard one of the following types of feedback:

1. Person-oriented feedback: "I'm disappointed in you."
2. Outcome-oriented feedback: "You didn't do that correctly."
3. Process-oriented feedback: "Maybe you could try a different way to stack the blocks?"
4. No feedback.

Children who received the process-oriented feedback were more likely to think of themselves as a good boy or girl, were more likely to think of themselves as happy, and were more likely to want to persist on the fictional task, for instance, trying again to make a neat stack or at least cleaning up the block pile. By contrast, children who received the person-oriented feedback scored lowest among the four groups on these measures. Even from this brief exercise, the latter group of children had started to internalize the message "if you don't do something well, there's something wrong with you," rather than the more constructive message received by students in the process-oriented group: "maybe you just need to try again to get it right."

Academic mindsets continue to influence how students do academically through elementary, middle, and high school. To demonstrate this, Dweck and colleagues Lisa Blackwell and Kali Trzesniewski designed an intervention to improve academic outcomes among lower-achieving middle school students in New York (Blackwell, Trzesniewski, & Dweck, 2007). Students were randomly assigned to one of two groups. Students in the treatment group received eight twenty-five-minute workshops focused on intelligence theory. The workshops encouraged a growth mindset by informing students that intelligence is malleable and can grow over time through hard work. Students in the control group received a series of workshops that did not focus on intelligence theory or mindsets. Teachers reported that students in the treatment group appeared more motivated after the workshops and had fewer disciplinary problems. The researchers also found that their academic achievement increased after the intervention.

Bringing this idea full circle, promoting growth mindsets can also counteract the effects of stereotype threat among Black college students. Psychologists Joshua Aronson, Carrie Fried, and Catherine Good (2002) designed a creative intervention to convey the malleability of intelligence to students. The authors recruited a group of Stanford undergraduates to take part in what was purportedly a pen pal mentoring program for middle school youth. One group of undergrads was assigned to write a letter to their pen pal which encouraged them to work hard in school even in the face of challenges they encountered in their lives. The researchers encouraged participants in this group to emphasize to their pen pals that intelligence has the capacity to grow "like a muscle" with ongoing mental exercise. The researchers went on to tell participants, "This message is especially important to get across to young, struggling students. If these students view intelligence as a fixed quantity, they may feel that they are incapable of learning if they encounter difficulty with their school work. If, however, students can be convinced that intelligence expands with hard work, they may be more likely to remain in school and put effort into learning." Another group of students was also assigned to write pen pal letters to middle school students, but instead of emphasizing the malleability of intelligence, students in this group were asked to impart on their students that there are many different types of intelligence and that students should continue to invest effort in school so that they can find their area of strength and confidence.

Relative to both the "multiple intelligences group" and a control group of students who did not write pen pal letters, students in the "intelligence is malleable" group experienced a range of positive outcomes. They were more likely to be more engaged in their coursework and experienced higher GPAs than students in either of the other groups. These improvements were most pronounced among Black students in the sample.

In a subsequent intervention, Good, Aronson, and colleague Michael Inzlicht (2003) investigated whether providing middle school students with *actual* peer mentors could help promote a growth mindset and counteract stereotype threat among female students. Working with a rural school district in Texas, the authors paired a sample of seventh-grade students in the district with college mentors from the University of Texas–Austin. The mentors had two in-person meetings with students, one that occurred in mid-November and the other at the end of January. They were additionally in touch with students via e-mail on a weekly basis. Across experimental groups the mentors provided students with advice on how to effectively study and on dealing with the transitional challenges of adapting to middle school. Mentors also helped students set up websites through which they could express creatively what they learned over the course of the mentoring.

For students who were assigned to the control group, mentors provided students with information about the dangers associated with drug use and how using drugs could negatively impact students' academic achievement. Students in the growth mindset group received messages from their mentors about the malleability of intelligence. As with the other interventions described in this chapter, the mentors provided students with information about how the brain works, along with additional web-based content that reinforced this information. Both females and males who were randomly assigned to the growth mindset group scored higher on subsequent math tests than students assigned to the control group, but the effects were particularly pronounced among female seventh graders. In fact, the mindset intervention was sufficient to erase the gender gap in math achievement which existed in the control group.

## SCALING MINDSET INTERVENTIONS

Just as with the social belonging interventions, Yeager, Walton, and colleagues are investigating how to bring growth mindset interventions to scale. Early findings suggest that mindset interventions can also generate meaningful improvements in student outcomes when implemented in the field and with a larger volume of students. In one intervention, for instance, the researchers conducted a mindset intervention with thirteen high schools from across the United States (Paunesku, Romero, Yeager, Walton, & Dweck, 2012). The researchers had teachers in the participating schools schedule two forty-five-minute sessions in their school's computer lab. Students assigned to the growth mindset treatment read an article about the brain's ability to grow and learn new things over time. Students were then asked to summarize what they had learned in their own words. Another group was asked to write advice for a student who was struggling and didn't think he was smart enough to succeed in school. Students in the control group participated in a computer-based activity that was unrelated to the malleability of intelligence. This brief mindset intervention led to a 14 percent increase in the share of courses that treatment group students completed with a satisfactory grade (for example, A, B, C). Gains were particularly pronounced in students' math classes; the share of courses for which students in the control group earned passing grades was flat over the same time period. The authors conducted a similar intervention with students enrolled in math courses at two community colleges and again found positive impacts of growth mindset interventions on whether students earned satisfactory grades in their math classes (Paunesku et al., 2012).

## GROWTH MINDSET INTERVENTIONS WITH TEACHERS

Of course, it is not only students' behavior that can be influenced by shifting their mindset—so too can their teachers. Teachers' own views about learning and intelligence can affect how they communicate with their students and, in turn, whether they reinforce a fixed or growth mindset in their pupils. In one experiment conducted by Dweck, Good, and colleague Aneeta Rattan, college undergraduates were randomly assigned to read an article about math intelligence, with one group's article presenting a growth mindset view of math learning and the other group's article presenting a fixed mindset outlook. After reading the article, participants in each group were asked to picture themselves as seventh-grade math teachers and describe how they would communicate with a struggling student. Participants who had read the fixed mindset article were more likely to believe that there were inherent limitations in the student's intelligence—that she simply wasn't "good at math." Rather than provide the student with concrete strategies for how she could improve her grade, participants who read the fixed mindset article were more likely to want to comfort her—as if not doing poorly on the math test was something she really couldn't do much about.

The malleability of teachers' views on intelligence also appears to hold up in the context of a field experiment. Stanford University doctoral student Susanna Claro (2014) conducted a mindset study with Chilean teachers who were participating in an online professional development course. Teachers were randomly assigned either to read an article about the structure of the brain and how to run effective meetings or to read an article about the malleability of intelligence and the importance of providing process-oriented feedback to students. Initial results indicate that teachers who received the latter treatment were more likely to complete the professional development course, particularly teachers whose baseline responses indicated they had more of a fixed mindset going into the intervention. Claro has yet to observe whether this increased engagement in the professional development course translated into improved student test scores, but I view this focus on promoting growth mindsets among teachers as a fruitful strategy for increasing student achievement.

The examples in this chapter offer an important lesson for policy makers, administrators, and teachers who could implement behavioral interventions to improve student educational outcomes. Many of the interventions described here—simplifying information, eliminating hassles associated with making important educational investments, prompting students to follow through on their intentions—may be only modestly effective if we do not simultaneously attend to the social factors that can influence student achievement. Students may not exert their full effort in educational experiences if they are anxious about confirming a negative stereotype about their group identity or if they believe that poor performance would indicate an inherent lack of capacity for academic success. Students may be reluctant to transition to new schools or may be less resilient in the face of academic challenges if they question their belonging in the first place. By actively countering stereotypes, teaching students about the malleability of intelligence, and promoting a sense of belonging, teachers can ensure that students get the most out of the opportunities available to them.

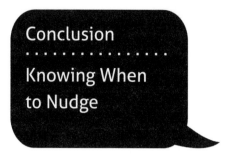

## Conclusion

## Knowing When to Nudge

I SET OUT TO BEGIN the conclusion for this book from 35,000 feet in the air. I mean this both figuratively and literally. I was on my way back from participating in a panel discussion at the College Board Forum. It was a beautiful day outside, the rugged beauty of the southwestern United States spread out below me for as far as the eye can see. The panel focused on Access to Opportunity, an initiative by College Board president David Coleman to help talented, economically disadvantaged students succeed academically. The initiative is also aimed at helping them attend well-matched, high-quality colleges and universities. The discussion made clear the stubborn persistence of socioeconomic disparities in both postsecondary access and attainment. It also reminded me how many smart and hardworking people are dedicating their lives to addressing these inequalities.

We don't lack for evidence-based solutions to help hardworking, low-income students access the best educational opportunities available to them. In the area of college access, we know from decades of research that offering students need-based financial aid increases the probability that students will succeed in college. We also know that improving academic readiness increases the likelihood that students will flourish once they get to college. The challenge is that these investments often require systemic and long-term change, and there are many students who need our help *now*. Furthermore, we see that there are academically college-ready students who have affordable options but who either are unaware of these options or struggle to overcome the financial and logistical hurdles necessary to access them.

Much of the discussion focused on the role of information and advising in helping students pursue academic opportunities that position them for success in college. We discussed many of the types of interventions I've profiled in this book: personalized text messaging campaigns; leveraging interactive technologies to connect students to individualized college advising; simplifying information about the college application process; proactively delivering application fee waivers to students to eliminate near-term cost barriers that may prevent them from making valuable educational investments. Insights from behavioral economics have informed the design of many of these interventions. The behaviorally informed strategies I've discussed throughout the book have made their way into the mainstream of efforts to improve college success. And as we've seen, these insights are increasingly guiding practice and policy throughout students' lives, from when children are barely old enough to toddle around all the way through high school and beyond.

I believe that the infusion of behavioral insights into educational policy and practice holds considerable potential for leveling the playing field. Affluent and educated families often have extensive personal experience and social networks they can draw on to make informed decisions about their children's education. At an even more basic level, they are more likely to have stable Internet connectivity they can use to access information or access to personal professional college advisors and test prep coaches. Targeted implementation of behavioral solutions can help compensate for this inequitable access to information and advice and can support students and families from economically disadvantaged backgrounds in making equally active and informed decisions about their education.

Like any innovation in education, however, behavioral economics does not offer a panacea. In fact, there are a series of open questions that we should consider as we assess how (and even whether) to try these interventions in other settings. One question that often comes up when I talk about my text messaging work, for instance, is whether these nudges are creating dependencies among the students we're serving. "You're texting them reminders about completing summer tasks and renewing their financial aid," someone will say. "Are you going to nudge them to hand in their homework in college? To search for summer internships? Where do you draw the line?" This is an important question, and one that I've wrestled with considerably. I believe that nudges are particularly important during critical junctures and transitions in students' educational trajectories: which school they attend; whether they take more rigorous courses; whether they complete required enrollment tasks or renew their financial aid. These decisions are often complex and hard to navigate. The choices students and families make can have long-lasting ramifications on how they do in school and whether they pursue additional education. I am strongly in favor of using behavioral nudges to support more informed decisions during these junctures. I am less certain about using nudges to encourage students— particularly as they get older—to follow through on more routine tasks like completing their homework. While I could see an argument in favor of doing so for a period of time when students transition to a new educational environment, it is also important to have an intentional phase-out plan, to help students develop the capacity to manage their time and follow through on these routines.

Another important question is whether there are diminishing returns on behavioral interventions. I believe that this is a particularly relevant question to ask with the mindset and social belonging interventions we looked at earlier. For instance, once students have been taught about the malleability of intelligence, is there value generated by repeating mindset interventions as the student advances throughout their education? Or if students participated in a social belonging intervention encouraging them to take more rigorous courses, would a social belonging intervention focused on the college transition be equally successful? To my knowledge researchers have not investigated the potential for diminishing returns of these interventions. However, because students are learning in a social context, it is possible that they would benefit from periodic growth mindset and social belonging refreshers throughout their education. After all, students may continue to encounter teachers who promote more of a fixed mindset outlook, which could undo gains from intelligence theory interventions in which students had previously participated. Similarly, pursuing high-quality educational opportunities may require underrepresented students to make a series of transitions to new environments when they go off to college: new schools; new peer groups; new residential environments. At each stage students may question whether they belong in the new setting.

It is also possible that certain types of behavioral interventions may actually have negative effects on students or their families. I think about this particularly in the context of the framing studies we looked at earlier. As the studies I described illustrated, emphasizing what students need to improve on appears to lead to greater effort than telling them what they're doing well. So too does framing opportunities in terms of avoiding losses rather than realizing potential gains. But taken to its logical extension, we might worry that only emphasizing what students need to improve on could, over time, have a demoralizing effect. That is, if we only point out where a student has fallen short without reminding them of their successes, we risk harm. Similarly, leveraging people's loss aversion in policy design may lead to greater effort and focus on the policy objective (for example, increasing students' test scores in the teacher incentive program) but may also have undesirable side effects. For instance, teachers' anxiety about losing their incentive payments might lead them to work toward improving test scores at the expense of other aspects of their relationship with students, which could lead to negative impacts for the teachers and students in the long run.

A further challenge with behavioral interventions is that our efforts to guide family decision making may lead to unintended consequences. This was evident in Jon Valant and Susanna Loeb's school choice intervention (Valant, 2014). Providing elementary school students and families with simplified information about their choices led to students attending higher-quality middle schools. However, the same intervention actually decreased the quality of high schools attended by those students. The authors speculate that this was a function of middle school students taking a more active role in school choice than they might have anticipated before the study began. Students may have been hesitant to select the highest-quality schools if they felt it would be too much work or if they thought they would struggle to succeed. They may also have been drawn to other information presented in the booklets which was negatively correlated with school performance. While the study design does not allow the authors to determine *why* the school choice booklets led middle school students to select lower-quality schools, their article does offer an important cautionary tale that people may not always respond to information in the way we expect.

The same is true of interventions that use descriptive social norms (sometimes unwittingly) to influence people's decisions. A famous example comes from the National Park Service's effort to reduce theft of petrified wood from Arizona's Petrified Forest National Park (Cialdini, 2003). Each month visitors to the park remove approximately one ton of petrified wood from the park, and needless to say, new petrified wood isn't being created very quickly. In an effort to reduce theft, the Park Service had prominently placed signs reporting on the level of theft. For instance, one sign read, "Your heritage is being vandalized every day by theft losses of petrified wood of 14 tons a year, mostly a small piece at a time." What the Park Service did not recognize was that these signs were communicating a message much different than what they intended: many people who come to the park steal petrified wood, so if you do too, it's not that big a deal. In other words, their signage was unintentionally establishing a descriptive norm that it was fairly normal to steal petrified wood during a visit to the park, desensitizing people from feeling bad if they did so themselves. Psychologist Robert Cialdini (2003) demonstrated that people were substantially more likely to steal wood when confronted with these kinds of signs rather than signs that more directly asked people not to remove wood from the park.

Concerns about establishing descriptive norms for undesired behaviors have also influenced how colleges and universities communicate with students about alcohol use. Rather than communicate about the number of students who binge drink and wind up in the hospital (a kind of "scared straight" approach), colleges such as Georgetown instead tried emphasizing that most students only have a few drinks when they go out. For instance, one ad features a picture of the Georgetown mascot and the following message: "Did you know . . . Most Hoyas have 0–4 drinks when they party?" (National Social Norms Institute, 2014).

One of the strengths of many of the behavioral interventions highlighted in this book is that they were evaluated in the context of randomized controlled trials (RCTs). This means that we can interpret the results as the unique effect of each intervention on students' educational outcomes, separate from all other factors that we know impact their behavior. This is an important point to emphasize; many studies in education mistake correlation for causality. For instance, if we observe that classrooms that use a certain type of math textbook tend to have higher scores on state math exams, we might be tempted to conclude that this particular textbook was more effective at promoting math achievement. However, it could also be the case that experienced teachers were more likely to seek out that textbook, and that it's really having an experienced teacher that leads to better scores. The rigor of this evidence notwithstanding, one drawback of these RCTs (mine included) is that they are often conducted in particular contexts that may not generalize to all educational settings. Even within the same study, interventions are sometimes effective in one place but not another. For instance, in my text messaging work to reduce summer melt, the text reminders led to substantial improvements in college enrollment in Lawrence and Springfield, Massachusetts, but had no effect on enrollment in nearby Boston. As a result, interventions that appeared highly effective during the research phase may have smaller impacts when implemented in other settings or on a larger scale.

A final cautionary note I will offer about applying behavioral insights in education is that they have the potential to be viewed as substitutes for existing investments in education. Behavioral interventions often have a creative appeal, and their low cost is alluring to educational leaders and policy makers who grapple with tight budgets and overflowing schools. The apparent "bang for the buck" of behavioral interventions should not be used as justification for scaling back spending on other important areas in education. After all, interventions to promote better decision making can only succeed if there are quality educational opportunities from which families can choose. What good would helping students and families complete the FAFSA be, for instance, if the federal government substantially scaled back Pell Grant funding? Would providing families with simplified information about school choice be worthwhile if districts didn't continue to invest in high-quality teachers?

## GUIDING PRINCIPLES FOR APPLYING
## BEHAVIORAL INSIGHTS IN EDUCATION

These words of caution notwithstanding, I believe that behavioral solutions have the potential to generate substantial and lasting improvements in educational achievement for economically disadvantaged students. I believe this in large part because families encounter such an intricate array of complex information and complicated processes throughout their educational trajectories. For behavioral interventions to be successful, the devil is often in the details. Because of this, we should conclude with concrete guidance for readers on how you can design behavioral interventions to help students and families you work with make active and informed decisions in education.

*Complete a Decision-Making Self-Diagnosis*

Whether you are a principal in a school, a director of a community-based organization, or an official at a state agency, many of you administer programs designed to expand educational opportunities for students in your community—a voucher program to defer costs of early childhood education for low-income families; a school choice program; the Advanced Placement (AP) or SAT program at your high school. Whatever the program, step back and evaluate how students and families learn about the program and what processes they need to go through to sign up and participate. The following are among the questions you may want to ask yourself:

- How is information about my program spread?
- How would students and families learn that this information is available? Do they use the communications channels through which I am delivering information?
- If I put myself in the shoes of students or parents, would this information make sense to me, or would I find some of the information or jargon confusing?
- What is the application procedure like? What do students and families have to do to sign up for the program?
- Are there near-term fees or hassles that might prevent someone from completing the application?

This self-diagnosis may reveal behavioral bottlenecks in the design of information or application procedures associated with your program which prevent families from taking advantage of the opportunities you are offering.

*Study Student Use Cases*

To understand why students and families make certain educational decisions, it's often very instructive to speak directly with the students and parents themselves. One group of students I suggest speaking with are those who appeared to make active and informed decisions. For instance, college access organizations might interview students who completed the FAFSA independent of any professional assistance to understand what resources they drew on or what motivated them to complete the application.

Just as beneficial is talking with students and families who didn't appear to make informed decisions. Earlier we looked at several of the summer melt interventions my colleagues and I developed to help college-bound high school graduates successfully enroll in college. What most informed this work was a series of interviews that my colleague Karen Arnold conducted with students in Providence, Rhode Island, who had paid deposits to attend college but who nonetheless reconsidered whether to attend in the months following high school graduation (Arnold, Fleming, DeAnda, Castleman, & Wartman, 2009). Arnold's illuminating interviews revealed the specific financial and procedural hurdles students encountered during the summer, and provided the direction for the subsequent interventions.

Just as product designers conduct focus groups in which they ask people to respond to specific products or services, ask students and their families to react to specific information or application procedures related to your program. If families don't appear to be choosing high-performing schools to send their children to, ask them to give feedback on the existing information that describes their school choices. Ask them about the application process. Were they intentionally leaving these higher-quality options on the table, or were other factors influencing their decisions?

These conversations, while time intensive and sometimes challenging to arrange, provide invaluable insight into how students and families currently make decisions and may highlight opportunities to tweak the process in ways that lead to improved student decisions.

### Seek Collaborators and Examples

Once you have a sense of the decision-making bottlenecks students and families may be facing, I encourage you to find collaborators who can help you design behaviorally informed interventions. There's a deceptive simplicity in the behavioral solutions I describe in this book. What may appear to be a straightforward set of text messages or articles on the malleability of intelligence often has a much deeper foundation of behavioral and psychological theory underneath it. Often researchers have invested substantial effort to design and implement these interventions in ways that are highly attuned to their target population and to the local context. This is not to say that you should not take the initiative to apply the insights from this book to design solutions for your students. I personally find the process of developing behavioral interventions to be a highly enriching and creative exercise. But I've also come to learn that the interventions I develop are much more likely to have a positive impact on students when I collaborate with other researchers who offer their own expertise and insight into helping students and families make informed decisions. Depending on where you are located, there may be faculty or students at nearby universities (a School of Education is a great place to start!) who would be eager for the chance to collaborate with educators on the design and implementation of behavioral interventions. Increasingly, there are also organizations like ideas42 which specialize in supporting schools to design effective solutions to behavioral obstacles.

In the event that your resources are limited and you are having trouble identifying collaborators, another approach is to seek out concrete examples from related behavioral interventions. Many of the published versions of the studies I highlight in this book provide the specific instruments they used in their interventions. For instance, my colleagues and I happily share the text message templates we've written with anyone who finds them useful, in the hope that they inform the design of similar campaigns.

### Get Lots of Feedback

Once you've designed an intervention, I strongly encourage you to seek out extensive feedback before putting it into the field. Most important is to prototype your materials with the students and families intended to benefit from the intervention. Ask for their candid feedback: How would they respond to intervention? Do they find the language authentic? Would the materials influence the decisions they would make? It is also worth asking a variety of colleagues in your school, organization, or agency. People who have worked with similar students and families probably have useful insights about how they approach decisions and may be able to help you refine and improve on the design of your intervention. Finally, seek out the feedback of researchers who study these interventions for a living. Even if faculty have limited time to provide this feedback, they may have graduate students who would gain a valuable learning experience from reviewing and providing constructive feedback on the design of a behavioral intervention.

While I have not personally explored this, I also wonder whether there are crowdsourcing sites through which you could get feedback on the design of your intervention materials. After all, there are online forums for everything else; maybe there's a group of budding behavioralists who would be more than happy to weigh in on the materials you've developed.

### Start Small and Evaluate

Probably the most important guidance I can offer is to start with a small group of students and intensively study how they respond to your intervention and whether it appears to influence their decisions, behaviors, and outcomes. If you have research capacity within your organization, I strongly encourage you to consider implementing your pilot as an RCT. As a former teacher and school administrator, I am sensitive to some educators' reluctance about RCTs. The idea of depriving some students of an intervention that other students are receiving can appear antithetical to our mission and purpose in education. But oftentimes we don't know whether interventions we are piloting are going to be successful—this was certainly true with the first text messaging intervention we ran. And in many cases, we don't have the resources to extend an intervention to all students who would potentially benefit from it. In these cases RCTs provide an equitable way for allocating slots while also generating rigorous evidence of the intervention's impacts. RCTs require substantial effort to design and implement, but I cannot underscore enough the returns I have observed from these studies: heightened support from internal leadership for the intervention; increased funding from internal operations or external sources; political and policy interest in expanding the intervention.

This was very much the course our summer melt work followed. The first summer melt intervention I conducted was in Providence, Rhode Island, with two school counselors reaching out to eighty recent high school graduates. The effects of this intervention were large enough to motivate other educational organizations to work with us to implement larger-scale versions of our counselor-outreach interventions. Positive results from these collaborations, in turn, built support for the other innovations we wanted to investigate—peer mentor outreach and personalized text message reminders among them. I am proud of the fact that tens of thousands of college-intending high school graduates across the country now receive additional advising support during the summer months, in part because of the strong foundation of evidence we created.

Starting small and rigorously evaluating behavioral interventions you design can do more than simply generate a similar evidence base. This iterative approach to design and evaluation can help you refine the quality of your intervention and identify variations and innovations that allow you to enhance the decision-making support you provide to students and their families.

## A FINAL WORD

It would be too dramatic for my tastes to say that we are entering the Behavioral Age in education, but I do believe that we have a tremendous opportunity in the coming years to help students and families make more informed decisions about their educational opportunities. First, we have a very strong foundation of research by behavioral economists and social psychologists on which we can draw to inform the designs of new interventions we develop. Many of these interventions have been applied in other policy arenas, but researchers are adapting them for the education sector with increasing frequency. Second, we have a rich array of data at our fingertips on which we can draw to make our interventions highly customized—and therefore more salient—for students and their families. These include detailed student-level data collected by schools and educational agencies, as well as extensive public data about the opportunities, policies, and programs that are available. Finally, we have a variety of communications channels we can use to deliver personalized, relevant, and just-in-time information. These same interactive technologies make it easier than ever to connect students to high-quality, individualized advising regardless of where the student lives.

Applying behavioral insights need not be the sole province of researchers and policy makers. My hope is that schools, community-based organizations, and state/federal education agencies can all draw on the lessons from this book to guide how they communicate with and support the students and families with whom they work. These investments in more active and informed decision making have the potential to reap substantial rewards. Whether at the preschool or collegiate level, attending a higher-quality school, pursuing more rigorous courses, or showing one's full potential on an exam can have a profound influence on later achievement. Behavioral interventions often cost little and can be relatively straightforward to implement, but they can nonetheless generate sizable and cascading effects by helping students and families overcome barriers that separate them from markedly improved learning environments. Over the long term we should continue to invest in the systemic changes necessary to ensure that every student in America has the highest-quality educational experience possible. But for the students who need our help *today*, behavioral economics offer a powerful set of insights that we can harness to improve their educational outcomes and their lives.

# Acknowledgments

I am deeply grateful to the contributions many people have made, not only to this book but more broadly to my understanding of how insights from behavioral economics and social psychology can be applied to education.

Three people deserve primary credit for this book (though they may not know how pivotal a role they played in its development). Professor Sarah Turner, one of my most valued mentors at the University of Virginia, is one of the first people who encouraged me to think about my research through a behavioral lens. Sarah also recommended me to write an essay on how behavioral insights could improve the design and delivery of college and financial aid information for a Gates Foundation project on behavioral insights and postsecondary success. Professor Sandy Baum, another invaluable mentor, accepted Sarah's recommendation and provided me the opportunity to do my first writing on behavioral economics and education. I also had the great privilege of coediting a volume with Sandy and Professor Saul Schwartz on behavioral insights and postsecondary success which built on the papers authored for the Gates project. Sandy introduced me to Beckie Supiano, an extraordinary reporter at the *Chronicle of Higher Education*, who wrote a profile on the paper I wrote for the Gates project, which caught the attention of my editor, Greg Britton, at Johns Hopkins University Press. Without this sequence of relationships and connections, this book would not have happened.

I am very grateful to Greg Britton for his vision for the potential of the book and his guidance and patience throughout the process of writing it. The structure and content of the book are immeasurably better because of his insights and thoughtful edits, and I will be forever grateful for his flexibility and support in seeing the book through to completion.

I am very fortunate to have had the assistance of two remarkable students, Katharine Meyer and Leah Remsen, in putting this book together. Katharine Meyer was the first person who I had read each chapter, and her feedback was both thorough and incredibly constructive. Katharine also ensured that I dotted all the i's and crossed all the t's, a not insignificant task or contribution, given my tendency to sometimes gloss over details. And Leah patiently and comprehensively assisted with assembling all the works cited for the book.

I would not have been in a position to write this book were it not for all that I have learned from my many research collaborators, faculty colleagues and mentors, and students. These include Karen Arnold, Chris Avery, Andrew Barr, Daphna Bassok, Peter Bergman, Eric Bettinger, Kelli Bird, Denise Deutschlander, Josh Goodman, Doug Harris, Cait Lamberton, Bridget Terry Long, Mike Luca, Zack Mabel, Laura Owen, Lindsay Page, Mark Robertson, Bruce Sacerdote, Barbara Schneider, Bill Skimmyhorn, Jon Smith, Zach Sullivan, Jon Valant, and Jim Wyckoff. I am also grateful to the staff at ideas42, from whom I have learned a great deal about behavioral economics, in particular from Katie Martin and Dan Connolly. And I am grateful to Maya Shankar and the rest of the White House Social and Behavioral Sciences Team for their engagement and insights.

None of my own research applying behavioral insights to improve postsecondary outcomes would have been possible without the close collaboration of many educational agencies. I feel very fortunate to have had the opportunity to collaborate with the following: Gabi Blumberg, Jessica Levin, Jon Schnur, and Bryden Sweeney Taylor at America Achieves, along with the tremendous staff at the College Advising Corps, College Possible, and Strive for College; Drew Scheberle and Gilbert Zavala at the Austin Chamber of Commerce; Dave Borger, Greg Johnson, and Andrew MacKenzie at Bottom Line; Steve Colon, Su Feldman, Jessica Howell, Mike Hurwitz, Cassie Larson, and Brooke White at the College Board; Lisa Zarin and Gregory Hill at College Bound–St. Louis; Nasim Kesharvez and Ginny Zawodny at the Community College of Baltimore County; Emily Froimson and Barbara Schmertz at the Jack Kent Cooke Foundation; Michael Lin and Ralph Passarella at Reify Health; Brian Kathman and the rest of the team at Signal Vine; Rosemary Hayes and David Yaskin at Starfish Retention Solutions; Alex Chewning, Erin Cox, and Bob Giannino-Racine at uAspire; Greg Cumpton, Chris King, and Heath Prince at the University of Texas–Austin Ray Marshall Center; Susan Carkeek, Patty Marbury, Steve Kimata, Lee Politis, and Greg Roberts at the University of Virginia; and Adam Green and Jessica Kennedy at the West Virginia Higher Education Policy Commission.

I am also very grateful for the generous financial support I have received from the following organizations: the Abell Foundation, Bloomberg Philanthropies, the Michael and Susan Dell Foundation, the Bill and Melinda Gates Foundation, the Heckscher Foundation for Children, the Institute for Education Sciences, the Lindback Foundation, the Lumina Foundation, the Kresge Foundation, the National Association of Student Financial Aid Administrators, the Spencer Foundation, the Texas Higher Education Coordinating Board, and the W. T. Grant Foundation.

Two English teachers, Mark Hershnik and Dan Mulvey, deserve special credit for inspiring my love of writing.

Last but not least, I am deeply appreciative of my family for supporting me throughout the process of writing this book. Throughout the highs and lows of writing, I always knew that I was coming home to the love and laughter that my wife, Celia, and children, Lila and Simon, offer daily. I owe my love of reading to my grandparents, Len and Anita Castleman; my writing ability to my mother, Janet Castleman; the example of writing a book to my aunt and uncle, Nancy Castleman and Marc Eisenson; and my appreciation of storytelling to my sister, Rachel Castleman.

# Notes

### INTRODUCTION. DECISIONS, DECISIONS

1. Throughout the volume I have changed names and identifying attributes of individual people to protect their privacy.

2. I draw on Thaler & Benartzi (2004) for this concept of tension between the impulses and desires of our present selves and the goals of our future selves.

### CHAPTER 1. THE COST OF COMPLEXITY

1. I borrow this analogy of the brain's accelerator and the brain's brake from Casey, Jones, and Somerville's (2011) highly informative article on the neurology of adolescent decision making.

2. Employees also had the third option of choosing their own retirement allocation instead of the Quick Enrollment option.

3. I am grateful to my colleague Daphna Bassok at the University of Virginia, whose insights and perspective informed my understanding of the decision-making challenges that families encounter when choosing day care options for their children.

4. My understanding of the expansion of and challenges associated with QRIS was informed by a final paper written by Amy Roberts for an education policy course I teach at the University of Virginia.

5. Unlike the other studies I report in this chapter, the university did not evaluate this intervention using experimental or quasi-experimental techniques, so it is possible that other factors contributed to this year-over-year decline in loan borrowing.

### CHAPTER 2. STARTING WITH THE STATUS QUO

1. In addition to information I gathered from the KIPP website, I am grateful to Anthony Hernandez, who shared his experiences as a teacher at a KIPP elementary school in Washington, DC.

2. Students who had been in the Kalamazoo Public Schools since ninth grade received a scholarship paying 65 percent of tuition at Michigan public colleges and universities.

3. For a summary of Reach Out and Read research, visit www.reachoutandread .org/FileRepository/Research_Summary.pdf.

### CHAPTER 3. ENCOURAGING ACTIVE DECISIONS

1. According to Surowiecki (2014), this focus on the importance of youth enrollment was misplaced. Of greater importance was ensuring that a sufficient volume of healthy people enrolled for a health care plan under ACA, regardless of their age (though, of course, young people do tend to be healthier than older people).

2. In Peru, customers who received the standard savings reminder did not save more than customers who did not receive any reminder.

3. To reiterate a point from chapter 1, lack of cognitive *bandwidth* should not be confused with a lack of cognitive *ability*.

4. The following example is drawn from Read, Loewenstein, and Kalyaranaman's (1999) experiment showing that people are more likely to choose "highbrow" movie rental options when they choose all at once which movies they will watch in the future rather than choosing each new movie after they have finished the prior one.

5. PBS *NewsHour* ran an informative story on the Stickk website, which can be viewed at www.pbs.org/newshour/bb/can-betting-online-help-save-money/.

6. Yes, I now live in Virginia, and yes, in my mind I'm still a lifelong New Englander.

7. This example is a variant on Tversky and Simonson's (1993) study comparing people's choices between $6 in cash and a fancy or cheap pen.

8. The authors also investigated how offering teachers individual versus group incentives affects students' performance.

### CHAPTER 4. FOLLOWING OUR FRIENDS—OR NOT

1. Social psychologists Steve Stroessner and Catherine Good created the website www.reducingstereotypethreat.org, which has a compendium of informative and accessible summaries of research studies that have investigated strategies to reduce stereotype threat. The papers I cite in the following paragraphs are largely drawn from this site.

2. I am indebted to Katharine Meyer for making this helpful observation.

# Works Cited

Allcott, H. (2011). Social norms and energy conservation. *Journal of Public Economics*, 95(9–10), 1082–1095.

Alman, A. (2014, March 11). Obama pushes Obamacare enrollment on "Between Two Ferns" with Zach Galifianakis. *The Huffington Post*.

Ambady, N., Paik, S. K., Steele, J., Owen-Smith, A., & Mitchell, J. P. (2004). Deflecting negative self-relevant stereotype activation: The effects of individuation. *Journal of Experimental Social Psychology*, 40, 401–408.

Ariely, D. (2008). *Predictably irrational: The hidden forces that shape our decisions*. New York, NY: HarperCollins.

Ariely, D., & Wertenbroch, K. (2002). Procrastination, deadlines, and performance: Self-control by precommitment. *Psychological Science*, 13(3), 219–224.

Arnold, K. C., Fleming, S., DeAnda, M., Castleman, B. L., & Wartman, K. L. (2009). The summer flood: The invisible gap among low-income students. *Thought and Action*, Fall, 23–34.

Aronson, J., Fried, C. B., & Good, C. (2002). Reducing the effects of stereotype threat on African American college students by shaping theories of intelligence. *Journal of Experimental Social Psychology*, 38, 113–125.

Avery, C., & Kane, T. J. (2004). Student perceptions of college opportunities: The Boston COACH program. In C. M. Hoxby (Ed.), *College choices: The economics of where to go, when to go, and how to pay for it* (pp. 355–394). Chicago, IL: University of Chicago Press.

Bailey, M. J., & Dynarski, S. M. (2012). *Gains and gaps: Changing inequality in U.S. college entry and completion*. National Bureau of Economic Research Working Paper No. 17633. Cambridge, MA: National Bureau of Economic Research.

Bartik, T. J., & Lachowska, M. (2014). The Kalamazoo Promise scholarship. *Education Next*, 14(2), 72–78.

Baum, S., Ma, J., & Payea, K. (2013). *Education pays*. New York, NY: The College Board.

Bergman, P. (2013). *Parent-child information frictions and human capital investment: Evidence from a field experiment*. Paper Presented at the National Bureau of Economic Research Economics of Education Program Meeting.

Bertrand, M., Mullainathan, S., & Shafir, E. (2004). A behavioral-economics view of poverty. *American Economics Review*, 94(2), 419–423.

Beshears, J., Choi, J. J., Laibson, D., & Madrian, B. C. (2012). *Simplification and saving.* National Bureau of Economic Research Working Paper No. 12659. Cambridge, MA: National Bureau of Economic Research.

Bettinger, E. P., Long, B. T., Oreopoulos, P., & Sanbonmatsu, L. (2012). The role of application assistance and information in college decisions: Results from the H&R Block FAFSA experiment. *The Quarterly Journal of Economics, 127*(3), 1205–1242.

Bird, K., & Castleman, B. L. (2014). *Here today, gone tomorrow? Investigating rates and patterns of financial aid renewal among college freshmen.* Center for Education Policy and Workforce Competitiveness Working Paper No. 25. Charlottesville, VA: University of Virginia.

Blackwell, L. S., Trzesniewski, K. H., & Dweck, C. S. (2007). Implicit theories of intelligence predict achievement across an adolescent transition: A longitudinal study and an intervention. *Child Development, 78*(1), 246–263.

Bleich, S. N., Barry, C. L., Gary-Webb, T. L., & Herring, B. J. (2014). Reducing sugar-sweetened beverage consumption by providing caloric information: How Black adolescents alter their purchases and whether the effects persist. *American Journal of Public Health, 104*(12), 2417–2424.

Bos, J. M., Berman, J., Kane, T. J., & Tseng, F. M. (2012). *The impacts of SOURCE: A program to support college enrollment through near-peer, low-cost student advising.* American Institutes for Research Working Paper.

Bowen, W. G., Chingos, M. M., & McPherson, M. S. (2009). *Crossing the finish line: Completing college at America's public universities.* Princeton, NJ: Princeton University Press.

Buehler, R., Griffin, D., & Ross, M. (1994). Exploring the "planning fallacy": Why people underestimate their task completion times. *Journal of Personality and Social Psychology, 67*(3), 366–381.

Bulman, G. (2012). *The effect of access to college assessments on enrollment and attainment.* Unpublished manuscript, Stanford University.

Carrell, S., & Sacerdote, B. (2013). *Late interventions matter too: The case of college coaching in New Hampshire.* NBER Working Paper No. 19031. Cambridge, MA: National Bureau of Economic Research.

Cascio, E. U., & Schanzenbach, D. W. (2014). *Expanding preschool access for disadvantaged children.* Washington, DC: Brookings Institution.

Casey, B., Jones, R. M., & Somerville, L. H. (2011). Braking and accelerating of the adolescent brain. *Journal of Research on Adolescence, 21*(1), 21–33.

Castleman, B. L. (Forthcoming). Prompts, personalization, and pay-offs: Strategies to improve the design and delivery of college and financial aid information. In

B. L. Castleman, S. Schwartz, & S. Baum (Eds.), *Decision making for student success*. New York, NY: Routledge Press.

Castleman, B. L., & Page, L. C. (2014). *Summer melt: Supporting low-income students in the transition from high school to college*. Cambridge, MA: Harvard Education Press.

Castleman, B. L., & Page, L. C. (2015). Summer nudging: Can personalized text messages and peer mentor outreach increase college going among low-income high school graduates? *Journal of Economic Behavior and Organization*, in press.

Castleman, B. L., & Page, L. C. (Forthcoming). Freshman year financial aid nudges: An experiment to increase FAFSA renewal and college persistence. *Journal of Human Resources*.

Castleman, B. L., Schwartz, S., & Baum, S. (2015). *Decision making for student success*. New York, NY: Routledge Press.

Chetty, R., Friedman, J. N., & Rockoff, J. E. (2011). *The long-term impacts of teachers: Teacher value-added and student outcomes in adulthood*. National Bureau of Economic Research Working Paper No. 17699. Cambridge, MA: National Bureau of Economic Research.

Chicago Tribune. (2014, March 11). Transcript: Obama's appearance on "Between Two Ferns."

Choi, J., Laibson, D., Madrian, B., & Metrick, A. (2003). *Passive decisions and potent defaults*. National Bureau of Economic Research Working Paper No. 9917. Cambridge, MA: National Bureau of Economic Research.

Chou, E. Y., & Murnighan, J. K. (2013). Life or death decisions: Framing the call for help. *PLoS One*, 8(3).

Cialdini, R. B. (2001). *Influence: Science and practice*. Boston, MA: Allyn & Bacon.

Cialdini, R. B. (2003). Crafting normative messages to protect the environment. *Current Directions in Psychological Science*, 12(4), 105–109.

Civic Enterprises. (2011). *School counselors literature and landscape review*. New York, NY: The College Board.

Claro, S. (2014). *Teachers' belief about malleable intelligence: A field experiment with Chilean elementary teachers*. Unpublished manuscript, Stanford University.

Cohen, G. L., & Garcia, J. (2005). I am us: Negative stereotypes as collective threats. *Journal of Personality and Social Psychology*, 89, 566–582.

Cohen, G. L., Garcia, J., Purdie-Vaughn, V., Apfel, N., & Brzustoski, P. (2009). Recursive processes in self-affirmation: Intervening to close the minority achievement gap. *Science*, 324, 400–403.

Complete College America. (2014). *Best practices: Guided pathways to success*. Retrieved November 14, 2014, from http://completecollege.org/strategies/#stratHolderPathwaySuccess.

Danaher, K., & Crandall, C. S. (2008). Stereotype threat in applied settings re-examined. *Journal of Applied Social Psychology, 38,* 1639–1655.

Delisle, J. (2014, August 4). Number of borrowers using income-based repayment doubles in one year. *New America Foundation.*

DiPerna, P. (2014). *2014 schooling in America survey.* Friedman Foundation for Educational Choice.

Dismukes, R. K. (2012). Prospective memory in workplace and everyday situations. *Current Directions in Psychological Science, 21*(4), 215–220.

Duckworth, A. L., Grant, H., Loew, B., Oettingen, G., & Gollwitzer, P. M. (2011). Self-regulation strategies improve self-discipline in adolescents: Benefits of mental contrasting and implementation intentions. *Educational Psychology, 31*(1), 17–26.

Dweck, C. (2006). *Mindset: The new psychology of success.* New York, NY: Random House.

Dynarski, S. M., & Scott-Clayton, J. E. (2006). The cost of complexity in federal student aid: Lessons from optimal tax theory and behavioral economics. *National Tax Journal, 59*(2), 319–356.

ElBoghdady, D. (2014, February 17). Student debt may hurt housing recovery by hampering first-time buyers. *The Washington Post.*

Federal Student Aid. (2014a). *Repayment plans.* Retrieved November 14, 2014, from www.direct.ed.gov/RepayCalc/dlindex2.html.

Federal Student Aid. (2014b). *Two-year official cohort default rates for schools.* Washington, DC: U.S. Department of Education.

Fernald, A., Marchman, V., & Weisleder, A. (2013). SES differences in language processing skill and vocabulary are evident at 18 months. *Developmental Psychology, 16*(2), 234–248.

Fishman, T. C. (2012, September 13). Why these kids get a free ride to college. *The New York Times Magazine.*

Fryer, R. G., Levitt, S. D., List, J., & Sadoff, S. (2012). *Enhancing the efficacy of teacher incentives through loss aversion: A field experiment.* NBER Working Paper No. 18237. Cambridge, MA: National Bureau of Economic Research.

Garber, M. (2014, June 16). Chili's has installed more than 45,000 tablets in its restaurants. *The Atlantic.*

Goldstein, N. J., Cialdini, R. B., & Griskevicius, V. (2008). A room with a viewpoint: Using social norms to motivate environmental conservation in hotels. *Journal of Consumer Research, 35*(3), 472–482.

Good, C., Aronson, J., & Inzlicht, M. (2003). Improving adolescents' standardized test performance: An intervention to reduce the effects of stereotype threat. *Applied Developmental Psychology, 24,* 645–662.

Goodman, S. (2012). *Learning from the test: Raising selective college enrollment by providing information.* Unpublished manuscript, Columbia University.

Grodsky, E., & Jones, M. T. (2007). Real and imagined barriers to college entry: Perceptions of cost. *Social Science Research, 36*(2), 745–766.

Grossman, J. B., & Tierney, J. P. (1998). Does mentoring work? An impact study of the Big Brothers / Big Sisters program. *Evaluation Review, 22*(3), 403–426.

Haggag, K., & Paci, G. (2014). Default tips. *American Economic Journal: Applied Economics, 6*(3), 1–19.

Harvard School of Public Health. (2014). *Obesity trends.* Retrieved November 14, 2014, from www.hsph.harvard.edu/obesity-prevention-source/obesity-trends/.

Hastings, J. S., & Weinstein, J. M. (2008). Information, school choice, and academic achievement: Evidence from two experiments. *The Quarterly Journal of Economics, 123*(4), 1373–1411.

Head, K. J., Noar, S. M., Iannarino, N. T., & Grant Harrington, N. (2013). Efficacy of text messaging-based interventions for health promotion: A meta-analysis. *Social Science & Medicine, 97,* 41.

Horn, L., Chen, X., & Chapman, C. (2003). *Getting ready to pay for college: What students and their parents know about the cost of college tuition and what they are going to find out.* Washington, DC: U.S. Department of Education, National Center for Education Statistics.

Hoxby, C. M., & Avery, C. (2012). *The missing "one-offs": The hidden supply of high-achieving, low income students.* NBER Working Paper No. 18586. Cambridge, MA: National Bureau of Economic Research.

Hoxby, C. M., & Turner, S. (2013). *Expanding college opportunities for high-achieving, low-income students.* Stanford, CA: Stanford Institute for Economic Policy Research.

Hurwitz, M., Smith, J., Niu, S., & Howell, J. (2014). The Maine question: How is 4-year college enrollment affected by mandatory college entrance exams? *Educational Evaluation and Policy Analysis, 20*(10), 1–22.

Iyengar, S. S., & Lepper, M. R. (2000). When choice is demotivating: Can one desire too much of a good thing? *Journal of Personality and Social Psychology, 79*(6), 995–1006.

Johnson, E. J., & Goldstein, D. (2003). Do defaults save lives? *Science, 302*(5649), 1338–1339.

Just, D. R., & Wansink, B. (2009). Smarter lunchrooms: Using behavioral economics to improve meal selection. *Choices,* 24.

Kamins, M. L., & Dweck, C. S. (1999). Person versus process praise and criticism: Implications for contingent self-worth and coping. *Developmental Psychology, 35*(3), 835–847.

Karlan, D., McConnell, M., Mullainathan, S., & Zinman, J. (2010). *Getting to the top of mind: How reminders increase saving.* NBER Working Paper No. 16205. Cambridge, MA: National Bureau of Economic Research.

Keating, D. P. (2004). Cognitive and brain development. In R. M. Lerner & L. Steinberg (Eds.), *Handbook of adolescent psychology* (2nd ed., pp. 45–84). New York, NY: Wiley.

Keckley, P. H., & Coughlin, S. (2012). *2012 survey of U.S. health care consumers: Five-year look back.* Washington, DC: Deloitte University Press.

King, J. E. (2004). Missed opportunities: Students who do not apply for financial aid. American Council on Education Issue Brief.

KIPP. (2014). KIPP public charter schools Knowledge is Power Program. Retrieved November 14, 2014, from www.kipp.org.

Kling, J. R., Mullainathan, S., Shafir, E., Vermeulen, L. C., & Wrobel, M. V. (2012). Comparison friction: Experimental evidence from Medicare drug plans. *The Quarterly Journal of Economics, 127*(1), 199–235.

Kofoed, M. S. (2013). *To apply or not apply: FAFSA completion and financial aid gaps.* Unpublished manuscript, University of Georgia.

Kraft, M. A., & Rogers, T. (2014). *Teacher-parent communication: Experimental evidence from a low-cost communication policy.* Paper Presented at the Society for Research on Education Effectiveness Spring Conference.

Lenhart, A. (2012). *Teens, smart phones, and texting.* Washington, DC: Pew Research Center.

Leventhal, H., Singer, R., & Jones, S. (1965). Effects of fear and specificity of recommendation upon attitudes and behavior. *Journal of Personality and Social Psychology, 2*(1), 20–29.

Lin, P. (2005). *When product variety backfires.* Cambridge, MA: Harvard Business School. Retrieved November 14, 2014, from http://hbswk.hbs.edu/item/4980.html.

Logel, C., Murphy, M., Walton, G., & Yeager, D. (2011). *College transition collaborative: At a glance.* Cornell University. Retrieved November 14, 2014, from http://sas.cornell.edu/sites/sas.cornell.edu/files/documents/College_Transition.pdf.

Long, B. T., & Mabel, Z. (2012). *Barriers to college success: Income disparities in progress to completion.* Unpublished manuscript.

Lorin, J. (2014, July 17). How Indiana University cut student debt. *Bloomberg Business Week.*

Lovelace, K., & Rosen, B. (1996). Difference in achieving person-organization fit among diverse groups of managers. *Journal of Management, 22*(5), 703–722.

Madrian, B. C., & Shea, D. F. (2001). The power of suggestion: Inertia in 401(K) participation and savings behavior. *The Quarterly Journal of Economics, 116*(4), 1149–1187.

Martinez, I. (2013). *The effects of nudges on students' effort and performance: Lessons from a MOOC.* Center for Education Policy and Workforce Competitiveness Working Paper No. 19. Charlottesville, VA: University of Virginia.

Milkman, K. L., Beshears, J., Choi, J. J., Laibson, D., & Madrian, B. C. (2011). Using implementation intentions prompts to enhance influenza vaccination rates. *Proceedings of the National Academy of Sciences, 108,* 10415–10420.

Moreno, C. (2014, August 1). Univision trumps English-language network giants, again. *The Huffington Post.*

Mullainathan, S. (2011). The psychology of poverty. *Focus, 28*(1), 19–22.

Mullainathan, S., & Shafir, E. (2013). *Scarcity: Why having so little means so much.* New York, NY: Times Books.

National Center for Education Statistics. (2012). Digest of education statistics, Table 392. Washington, DC: U.S. Department of Education.

National Center for Education Statistics. (2013). Digest of education statistics, Tables 384 and 387. Washington, DC: U.S. Department of Education.

National Social Norms Institute. (2014). The National Social Norms Institute. Retrieved November 14, 2014, from www.socialnorms.org.

Nickerson, D. W., & Rogers, T. (2010). Do you have a voting plan? Implementation intentions, voter turnout, and organic plan making. *Psychological Science, 21*(2), 194–199.

Pallais, A. (Forthcoming). Small differences that matter: Mistakes in applying to college. *Journal of Labor Economics.*

Paunesku, D., Romero, C., Yeager, D., Walton, G., & Dweck, C. (2012). *Changing mindsets to raise achievement: Evidence from the Stanford university project for education research that scales.*

Phillips, L., & Stuhldreher, A. (2011). *Kindergarten to College (K2C): A first-in-the-nation initiative to set all kindergartners on the path to college.* Washington, DC: New America Foundation.

PR Newswire. (2006). *New Year's resolutions: Easier to make than to keep.* Retrieved November 14, 2014, from www.prnewswire.com/news-releases/new-years -resolutions-easier-to-make-than-to-keep-55107147.html.

The Project on Student Debt. (2013). *Student debt and the class of 2012.* Washington, DC: The Institute for College Access & Success.

Rasmussen Reports. (2011). *75% say exercise is important in daily life.* Retrieved November 14, 2014, from www.rasmussenreports.com/public_content/lifestyle /general_lifestyle/march_2011/75_say_exercise_is_important_in_daily_life.

Ray, B. (2014, July 3). Could text messages to parents help close the "word gap"? *New America Foundation.*

Reach Out and Read. (2014). *Reach out and read.* Retrieved November 14, 2014, from www.reachoutandread.org/.

Read, D., Loewenstein, G. F., & Kalyanaraman, S. (1999). Mixing virtue and vice: The combined effects of hyperbolic discounting and diversification. *Journal of Behavioral Decision Making, 12,* 257–273.

Redelmeier, D. A., & Shafir, E. (1995). Medical decision making in situations that involve multiple alternatives. *Journal of the American Medical Association, 273*(4), 302–305.

Rich, M. (2014, June 24). Pediatrics group to recommend reading aloud to children from birth. *The New York Times.*

Risley, T. R., & Hart, B. (1995). *Meaningful differences in the everyday experience of young American children.* Baltimore, MD: Paul H. Brookes Publishing Co.

Rockoff, J. E., Staiger, D. O., Kane, T. J., & Taylor, E. S. (2010). *Information and employee evaluation: Evidence from a randomized intervention in public schools.* National Bureau of Economic Research Working Paper No. 16240. Cambridge, MA: National Bureau of Economic Research.

Rogers, T., Milkman, K., John, L., & Norton, M. I. (Forthcoming). Making the best laid plans better: How plan-making increases follow-through. *Behavioral Science and Policy.*

Ross, R., White, S., Wright, J., & Knapp, L. (2013). *Using behavioral economics for postsecondary success.* New York, NY: ideas42.

San Francisco Office of Financial Empowerment. (2014). *Kindergarten to College.* Retrieved November 14, 2014, from http://sfofe.org/programs/k-to-c.

Scott-Clayton, J. (2015). The shapeless river: Does a lack of structure inhibit students' progress at community colleges? In B. L. Castleman, S. Schwartz, & S. Baum (Eds.), *Decision making for student success.* New York, NY: Routledge Press.

Scrivener, S., & Weiss, M. J. (2013). *More graduates: Two-year results from an evaluation of accelerated study in associate programs (ASAP) for developmental education students* (Policy Brief). New York, NY: MDRC.

Shih, M., Pittinsky, T. L., & Trahan, A. (2006). Domain-specific effects of stereotypes on performance. *Self and Identity, 5,* 1–14.

Smith, J., Pender, M., & Howell, J. (2013). The full extent of student-college academic undermatch. *Economics of Education Review, 32,* 247–261.

Solar City. (2014). *U.S. homeowners on clean energy: A national survey* (Poll Results). SolarCity.

Steele, C. M., & Aronson, J. (1995). Stereotype threat and the intellectual test performance of African Americans. *Journal of Personality and Social Psychology, 69*(5), 797–811.

Steinberg, L. (2008). A social neuroscience perspective on adolescent risk-taking. *Development Review, 28,* 78–106.

Steinberg, L., Cauffman, E., Woolard, J., Graham, S., & Banich, M. (2009). Are adolescents less mature than adults? Minors' access to abortion, the juvenile death penalty, and the alleged APA "Flip-flop." *American Psychologist, 64,* 583–594.

Stephens, N. M., Hamedani, M. G., & Destin, M. (2014). Closing the social-class achievement gap: A difference-education intervention improves first-generation students' academic performance and all students' college transition. *Psychological Science, 25*(4), 943–953.

Stockwell, M. S., Kharbanda, E. O., Martinez, R. A., Vargas, C. Y., Vawdrey, D. K., & Carmago, S. (2012). Effect of a text messaging intervention on influenza vaccination in an urban, low-income pediatric and adolescent population: A randomized controlled trial. *JAMA, 307*(16), 1702–1708.

Stricker, L. J., & Ward, W. C. (2004). Stereotype threat, inquiring about test takers' ethnicity and gender, and standardized test performance. *Journal of Applied Social Psychology, 34,* 665–693.

Surowiecki, J. (2014, March 31). Young, healthy, and not so important for Obamacare. *The New Yorker.*

Thaler, R. H., & Benartzi, S. (2004). Save more tomorrow: Using behavioral economics to increase employee saving. *The Journal of Political Economy, 112*(1), 164–187.

Tout, K., Starr, R., Soli, M., Moodie, S., Kirby, G., & Boller, K. (2010). *Compendium of quality rating systems and evaluations.* Washington, DC: Office of Planning, Research and Evaluation—Department of Health and Human Services.

Tversky, A., & Simonson, I. (1993). Context-dependent preferences. *Management Science, 39*(10), 1179–1189.

U.S. Department of Education. (2014). *Department of Education fiscal year 2014 congressional action table.* Washington, DC: U.S. Department of Education.

U.S. Department of Health and Human Services. (2014a). *Chapter 2: Physical activity has many health benefits.* Washington, DC: Department of Health and Human Services.

U.S. Department of Health and Human Services. (2014b). *Health insurance marketplace: March enrollment report* (Issue Brief). Washington, DC: Department of Health and Human Services.

U.S. Department of Health and Human Services. (2014c). *Health insurance marketplace: Summary enrollment report for the initial annual open enrollment period* (Issue Brief). Washington, DC: Department of Health and Human Services.

U.S. Government Accountability Office. (2011). *Disadvantaged students: School districts have used Title I funds primarily to support instruction.* Washington, DC: U.S. GAO.

Valant, J. (2014). Governed by choice: How school choosers and the public assess school quality and respond to information. Doctoral dissertation, Stanford University.

Vitality. (2014). *A six month randomized control trial reveals promising early results.* Retrieved November 14, 2014, from www.vitality.net/research_harvard.html.

Walton, G. M., & Cohen, G. L. (2007). A question of belonging: Race, social fit, and achievement. *Journal of Personality and Social Psychology, 92*(1), 82–96.

Walton, G. M., & Cohen, G. L. (2011). A brief social-belonging intervention improves academic and health outcomes of minority students. *Science, 331*(6023), 1447–1451.

White, K. M., Hogg, M. A., & Terry, D. J. (2002). Improving attitude-behavior correspondence through exposure to normative support from a salient in-group. *Basic and Applied Social Psychology, 24,* 91–103.

The White House. (2013). *First Lady Michelle Obama speaks on the power of education.*

York, B. N., & Loeb, S. (2014). *One step at a time: The effects of an early literacy text messaging program for parents of preschoolers.* Center for Education Policy Analysis Working Paper. Stanford, CA: Stanford University.

# Index